Beat Binary Options

Winning Financial Betting Strategies for Today's Markets

Drew Kasch

© 2014 by AndrewKaschPublishing.com

All Rights Reserved. No part of this publication may be reproduced in any form or by any means, including scanning, photocopying, or otherwise without prior written permission of the copyright holder.

Disclaimer and Terms of Use: The Author and Publisher have strived to be as accurate and complete as possible in the creation of this book, notwithstanding the fact that he does not warrant or represent at any time that the contents within are accurate due to the rapidly changing nature of the Internet. While all attempts have been made to verify information provided in this publication, the Author and Publisher assume no responsibility for errors, omissions, or contrary interpretation of the subject matter herein. Any perceived slights of specific persons, peoples, or organizations are unintentional. In practical advice books, like anything else in life, there are no guarantees of personal results. This book is not intended for use as a source of legal, business, accounting, medical, or financial advice. All readers are advised to seek services of competent professionals in the legal, business, accounting, medical, and finance fields. Furthermore, what works for some people may not work for others. Following the advice given in this book may result in unintended consequences in your life and the author and publisher assume no responsibility for that. Pursue the contents of this book at your own risk.

Problem gamblers should seek professional help and stay the heck away from online betting and trading sites. No system or strategy will work for problem gamblers, anywhere, anyplace – including binary options sites.

ISBN-13: 978-1496168023

ISBN-10: 149616802X

Table of Contents

Introduction 1

What Sites to Trade At 7

The Challenges: Why It's So Hard to Win Consistently 11

The Solutions: How You Can Beat the Game 19

Site Orientation and Wager Type Analysis 29

Directional and Non-Directional Trading Tactics 37

Choosing a Market and Strategy 49

Strategy #1: Mastering the Intraday Breakout 57

Strategy #2: High-Odds Big Picture Positioning 79

Strategy #3: One-Touch Reversal 91

Strategy #4: The Index Straddle & Range 105

Strategy #5: Price Tracking for Value 123

Developing Your Binary Options Business Plan 135

Onward and Upward to Real Trading 143

About the Author 164

Forethought

In the nine years since the first edition of this book was published, there have been many changes in the fixed-odds binary options landscape. Most of these changes have ultimately been positive for the trader, as competition from an ever-widening pool of brokers creates value for the player that just wouldn't be there otherwise. The opportunities for personalizing a winning strategy and using it as a springboard for trading success have never been better.

In this fourth edition, much-needed updates and revisions were made to the five core trading strategies, some of which were in response to different maximum payouts for certain types of wagers. In addition, important new sections have been added. The goal is to teach the reader how to find high-odds trading setups in any market – and, correspondingly, how to finagle the best possible edge at the binary options sites by identifying the wager that holds the most value for the situation.

Please note this book is specifically about trading **fixed-odds** binary options (European style, non-U.S. regulated). There are plenty of sites where U.S. citizens can play these, but let the reader be aware that we will not be addressing the CBOE-regulated, 0-100 style options contracts in this work. We're talking *One-Touch bets* and the like here. Sometimes this type of trading is referred to as *financial betting*.

Truth be told, beating binary options is easier than being a winning trader at a traditional broker. This is because the amount risked is built into the trade right at the outset. That means you are automatically disciplined to obey your stop-loss points, which are determined by the size of your bet. Do you realize this eliminates the sole reason most failed traders blew their accounts out? There's no way for one bad trade to get away from you and end your career.

It is entirely possible to start with $100 and build it into $10,000 over time with this style of trading. I said possible, not easy. Once binary options are mastered, the trader can then graduate to traditional brokerage accounts, make a few adjustments, and continue to compound wealth. The valuable lessons in risk-control learned while trading binary options will (hopefully) then keep the trader from becoming derailed by a devastating loss in any single trade. This book will help you make the transition to traditional broker accounts as well.

Developing the skills taught in the following pages will allow you to join the ranks of the elite few. Not just the small percentage of players who actually win at trading binaries, but those fortunate and wealthy professionals who trade for a living.

Introduction

There is nothing quite so satisfying as closing a winning trade. Ironically, this is exactly what causes many traders to eventually fail. The winning trade is addicting. It makes us want to put on another trade right away, and maybe fudge on our entry set-up requirements just a bit, so we can have that feeling again. Ah, that feeling! It conjures up images of quitting our job and buying a big house in the harbor with a boat dock. We can even calculate how wealthy we will become in just a few short years by adding a compounding effect to the percentage gain we just made.

A losing trade, on the other hand, can ruin our mood entirely. We tend to conclude that trading can't be beat as a feeling of resignation comes over us. We envision ourselves stuck in a dead-end job until our seventies and then scraping by on a tiny social security check, slowly bleeding away our savings until we finally die in poverty.

Successful traders manage to free themselves of these feelings on both winning and losing trades. All they care about is that their account equity grows steadily in the larger time frame. They treat trading as a business and completely accept losing trades as a necessary cost of doing business. Cultivating this attitude will be largely responsible for your success as a trader, regardless of the trading vehicles you use.

This manual will show you how to run a successful binary options trading operation and use it as a catalyst for financial freedom. You will learn a handful of financial betting strategies that can give you an edge, along with the optimal position sizing tactics that will allow you to maximize this edge. Most importantly, you will learn how to detach yourself emotionally from the outcome of any particular wager. Thus you will be able to treat the building of your financial security as a business – one that provides a clear vision of success and lets you sleep soundly at night.

Why Binary Options?

There is only one really good reason to be a fixed odds binary options trader: Because you currently don't have sufficient funds to operate a "real" trading account with a broker. A binary options account is simply a poor man's trading account. As such, it should be your goal to use it as a springboard to build up an account size sufficient for funding a real trading account, which you will then ultimately use to become wealthy.

Introduction

That is the theme and objective of this book. Not just to show you a few tips and tricks for making winning financial bets, but to give you a roadmap for becoming wealthy in your lifetime starting with very little capital. Although the exact steps for locating, entering, and exiting winning financial bets may differ significantly from doing the same with a stock, options, futures, or currency trading account, the general principles are the same. If you can win at one, then you should have little trouble making the adjustments for succeeding at any of the others.

There is one notable exception to my assertion that a binary options account will outgrow its usefulness when your trading capital reaches a certain size, and it has to do with the *Intraday Breakout Strategy* taught in this course. This strategy may still be useful to you even after you have graduated to a brokerage-based trading account. There really isn't a tradable equivalent to the intraday bets that are offered on many of the binary options sites, because of their "all or nothing" aspect. For this reason, I still keep a binary options account as a supplement to my day trading activities. (The Intraday Breakout Strategy is only usable by those able to keep an eye on the market for most of the trading session. Don't worry if this requirement excludes you, as there are ample lower-maintenance strategies in the following chapters to ensure your success.)

Even so, the intraday breakout strategy does have its limitations once your trading capital has reached a certain point. This is mainly due to the proper risk control principles you will be employing. It would be great if we could compound our capital at a site like Binary.com indefinitely, but this would be foolish. Our funds are not insured there. They are reasonably safe at Binary.com, as this site is well-established and backed by Regent Pacific Group, a large financial company that is traded on the Hong Kong stock exchange. Even so, if you have $100,000 in total trading capital it would not be prudent to keep more than $10,000 there. One day they could suddenly declare insolvency and we would have no recourse. (Other binary options sites seem reasonably safe as well, including many that accept U.S. citizens – but none quite as safe as Binary.com.) So our ultimate wealth will not come from trading binary options. But many of us can use this account to get our financial well-being off the launching pad, going from say $500 to $10,000 or so, at which time it would be appropriate to start trading with a broker.

Of course, many brokers will accept a much smaller initial account size. Heck, $1,000 will get you a brokerage account trading equities, options, spot currencies, or even commodity futures these days. But is it wise to open a brokerage account with such a small amount? In a word, no. A high percentage of small accounts opened with brokers lose the entire balance very quickly. There are a number of factors working against small accounts, not the least of which is a higher commission per trade ratio. You are better off with a binary options account until you have $10,000 or more to work with. That's the magic number. At that point, you should probably look to switch to a broker-based trading account of some sort, but not before then.

So that's the why of financial betting. We can start to employ a winning trading methodology with very little starting capital, even making as little as $5 bets in the beginning. By learning to become a winning trader with a small bankroll, we are forming good habits that will allow us to build real wealth over time. There is no need to risk more than a paltry sum in the beginning, and no need to abandon good risk control principles along the way. A binary options trading account is the perfect place for learning, honing, and perfecting our craft.

What You Will Learn in this Manual

There are five timelessly-effective financial betting strategies taught in this course. Mastering any one of them can make all the difference in your financial future, even if you are starting with only $100 right now. Anyone who has a mind to should be able to get good with at least two or three of them. The ==psychology of becoming a winning trader is by far the most important thing you can learn==. After that, your potential will only be limited by what you dare yourself to accomplish.

Beat Binary Options

What Sites to Trade At

Binary options trading sites come and go. The most stable of them, in my opinion, is **Binary.com**. The first couple of editions of this book were written specifically for a site known as *BetonMarkets* (many of you will be familiar with them, no doubt) that has now been absorbed by Binary.com. **Regent Pacific Group** is the company behind both these sites. They have a long track record of being solvent, and their financial status can be viewed quarterly when they file their public reports. Good luck finding that kind of transparency with anyone else.

Other sites are less stable. Some of them have better reputations than others. I have put together a very partial list, below, of additional "reputable" binary options trading sites at the time of this writing (in the spring of 2014). As the years go by, no doubt some will no longer exist – but Regent Pacific Group will doubtless still have a binary options site running, whether it is still called Binary.com or something else.

The thing to always keep in mind is the principle, not the specific details. Binary options sites are a modern reality, extremely popular in European markets, and thus are here to stay regardless of what USA regulators might say. It doesn't really matter what site you trade at; only that they have a good reputation for reliability and that they offer attractive and consistent trading contracts. If you are using sites other than Binary.com, it might be a good idea to spread the funds out over several different accounts as an extra layer of safety.

Before choosing a site, I recommend doing your own homework first. Do an internet search for *Binary Options Site Reviews* and other similar queries. But be aware of the scam review sites that are only there to post their affiliate links! Instead, find the true review sites that list both the reputable and no-so-reputable sites, which include user feedback (especially a public forum). In this manner you can get a feel for the current marketplace.

Reputable Binary Options Sites as of Spring 2014

Binary.com (highly recommended, but no USA accounts)
OptionsXO
OptionsBit
EZTrader
MarketsWorld
TradeRush
uBinary
GTOptions
OptionTime
Top Option
24 Option
Redwood Options
StockPair

Many of the above sites do accept USA traders at the time of this writing.

Please note I have omitted betting exchanges such as Betfair, Intrade, Matchbook, etc. which also offer financial markets contracts. These operate differently than the European-style, fixed-odds "financial-betting" binary options and thus require different strategies. Those contracts are priced from 0-100 and expire at either 0 or 100, like the CBOE binary contracts. At betting exchanges, it's more about getting an edge against the other players and you can even assume the role of the house if you want. If you are interested in specific strategies tailored to that type of trading, see my book *How to Milk the Betting Exchange Cash Cow*.

Successful fixed-odds financial betting at European-style binary options sites, such as those listed above, is about learning to trade well enough to beat the financial markets themselves. The big markets will always be around, so this is a skill worth developing. But it's also about learning to take advantage of the most attractive types of wagers available at these sites, which sometimes offer irresistibly attractive payouts on certain trades. This is what we'll be doing in the following pages. Master these skills and no one will ever be able to take them away from you, regardless of the political environment you find yourself surrounded by. Let's get started...

Beat Binary Options

The Challenges: Why It's So Hard to Win Consistently

Winning consistently enough to show steady monthly profits is not easy. If it were, the binary options sites would not be in business. Obviously, everyone is not winning. In fact, only a very small percentage of their customers are beating this game. You are going to be one of them. In order to join this elite group, you first must understand why almost everyone else loses.

What I find particularly entertaining is that the "gurus" in the various binary options trading forums can't even beat the game. Some of these people actually charge for their betting signals. What's even funnier is that some of them do have paying customers. This kind of thing was prevalent at the old BetonMarkets site forum (BetonMarkets was the original binary options site pioneer). Yet, if you clicked on the guru's public link to check their performance record, you would inevitably find that either they had a very small account and had been losing, or they had turned off the feature that allowed their results to be publicly-viewable. If they turned off their public link, you can be certain they were losing, as anyone with a winning record that is trying to recruit paying customers for their signals would be showing it off.

There used to be betting clubs, too. There were never any betting clubs with a decent winning record, either.

Right about now, you're probably wondering how in the world anyone could possibly win at this. And rightly so. If the gurus and clubs couldn't beat the game, how can anyone? Is it even possible to do? Let's explore that question a little before arriving at the answer.

Random Walk Theory

The first question we should think about is whether or not the markets themselves can be beaten. The *Random Walk Theory* says no. The supporters of this theory include many highly-educated, brilliant mathematical minds. Random walkers believe the price movements of financial markets happen randomly, and, therefore, no system or strategy devised will show a long-run profit. Traders that have impressive performance records are simply those that are temporarily on the positive side of the distribution curve (in other words, they have just been lucky so far). Eventually, every trader should end up down the exact amount that their commission cost. If there were no commissions, then you would be playing a zero sum game where the short-term results cannot be attributed to skill. All the fundamentals, charts, and indicators in the world are just a waste of time and effort.

How's that for a bleak view of things? Now don't go and get all despondent on me, because it just so happens that the random walkers are wrong. You'd think those brilliant mathematical minds would realize the undeniable existence of a handful of successful traders with long track records disproves the random walk theory. And there are more than just a handful of these highly profitable traders – read the *Market Wizards* series of books if you need convincing. Furthermore, way too many beginning traders fail spectacularly by blowing out their entire accounts for the markets to be operating randomly. With something like 90% of all new traders failing rather quickly, the odds are obviously much higher against a brand new trader succeeding than what could be accounted for by the random distribution of results. The fact that there are no gurus in the forums that show a sustained profitability for any reasonably long period of time further supports this notion.

It might seem that I am arguing the markets are even more difficult to beat than a random walk. In a way, I am. That creates a skew. If there is a skew, we can simply take the other side of it. In other words, we can take the opposite side of the trades the 90% of new traders who are failing are making. Unfortunately, it's not quite that simple, but that's the general idea. If the odds are anything other than even we can put the winning percentage on our side, and as a successful trader that is the basis of our winning methodology.

The reason so many smart people believe in the Random Walk Theory is because they are mostly correct. Market movements in reality are mostly random, but are skewed by a trending element and are frequently interrupted by short periods of extreme non-randomness. It is those pockets, along with the trending element, that create our opportunity for profit.

Black-Scholes Option Pricing Model

Traditional option trading is one area of the market where the professionals have a clearly defined advantage over the gamblers, hopers, and dreamers in the short run. This is because they sell overpriced options to those looking for a big score. The reason they can do this is because the dreamers will pay too much premium in their pursuit. The gamblers are buying overpriced options and the professionals are selling them. The pros wouldn't bother selling the options unless they could get an edge by selling overvalued premium, so the dreamers have no choice but to pay for it. (It should be noted that most option sellers eventually fail as well, even though they have an edge. The main reason is from lack of a well-conceived business plan, as they are ill-prepared for the tiny percentage of positions that hit against them for huge scores.)

Option values are calculated by pricing models, the most popular is known as Black-Scholes. Maybe this model produces accurate values, and then again maybe not. But it is a uniform formula used in the options market, so for our purposes it really doesn't matter. We are not going to invent a better model and then exploit the differences, although a small handful of very successful options traders do just that. What we are initially concerned with is getting an edge in our financial betting, and we only care about the Black-Scholes option pricing model because that is what the binary options sites use as a basis for figuring the pricing on the wagers they offer.

The factors that drive option prices are also what determine the wager prices at the binary options sites. The most important of these factors is the **volatility** of the underlying security. When a security is volatile *One-Touch* bets pay less, and when a security is docile the *Range* plays pay next to nothing. So it's a critical factor in hunting for attractive financial wagers.

The binary options sites are very much like option sellers and their customers are very much like options buyers. Since over 90% of option traders lose money, this is a very lucrative business. They are a modern day "bucket shop" with one notable distinction: They can limit their risk by only offering wagers they are comfortable with.

Binary Options Pricing & Commissions

The wagers offered on the binary options sites are loosely calculated from the Black-Scholes model. Then commissions to the site are figured in, as if option pricing alone wasn't tough enough to beat. These commissions take several forms depending on the wager type. Usually they are either an increase in the cost of what the bet is currently "worth" by the options model calculation, or a spread that is assigned to the wager that the underlying security has to beat (this is why financial betting in the U.K. sometimes goes by the term *spread betting*).

The commissions are a formidable opponent to our success and cannot be taken lightly. The bets we make must have enough of an edge to cover the commissions and still leave us a profit for the average result. Obviously, anyone making frivolous wagers will have no chance at coming out ahead.

It is my belief that the pricing is sometimes further skewed to allow the binary options broker to lay the wagers off in the financial markets at a profit if they so choose. If I am correct, this is a further hurdle that must be cleared. No wonder none of the gurus or betting clubs could rack up a decent return.

The Trend is Binary Option Broker's Friend

A One-Touch bet in the direction of a trending market will usually be priced significantly worse than the same One-Touch bet in the opposite direction of the trend. For example, the day I wrote this paragraph the U.S. stock markets have been trending strongly downward over the last few days and weeks. A six trading-day one touch bet at Binary.com on the NASDAQ at 75 points below its current level is returning 167%, but 75 points above the current level pays 235%. That's too big of a difference even to be accounted for by options premiums being skewed in the direction of the trend.

Could it be that Binary.com is playing the trend? Draw your own conclusion, but one thing is for sure: If playing the trending element in financial markets is the best way to escape the random walk, then it would sure seem like someone is trying to take that edge away from us as well.

Conclusion

It's tough! You have to find trade setups in the isolated pockets of non-random market movements that have a high enough chance of being profitable to cover the binary option broker's added commission, plus deal with a possible further skew from inflated option premium built into the pricing, plus possibly even an extra edge allowing the binary broker the ability to lay the wager off profitably.

But all this **can** be done. ==Value can be found in certain types of bets at certain times.== To be a winning financial bettor, you must stick to those and avoid all the others. Turn to the next chapter to learn how we can conquer these challenges and go on to design a winning binary options trading methodology.

Beat Binary Options

The Solutions: How You Can Beat the Game

As you are no doubt aware of by now, the challenge of beating binary options for a steady monthly return is a formidable one. You can't just start making bets that look good to you. You must have a carefully thought-out approach that you are adhering to, one that gives the bets you make an edge so your average expected result is positive. Achieving this isn't as difficult as it sounds, fortunately. It's just not the way most people who play this game want to bet. That's why so few people have a winning record.

The answers to the problems facing us as a binary options trader are found by employing a combination of trading skills, betting savvy, and money management (position sizing). All three must integrate well in order to maximize our results. You already know what we're up against – a statistical, mathematical robot that never makes elementary mistakes. So we can't, either. One dumb mistake per month is enough to turn a winning trader into a loser.

If you open an account, log on and start making bets, you are throwing money away. You need a well-conceived plan of attack and a specific methodology for locating attractive wagers if you want to succeed. Many of the wager types offered on some of the binary options sites aren't even worth considering. There are only five that are utilized in the strategies taught in this manual. They are:

One Touch (price touches any time before expiration)

No Touch Expiration (price never touches before expiration)

Range Expiration (within defined range at expiration)

Barrier Expiration (price is above or below at expiration)

Intraday Expiration Wagers (of all types and timeframes)

Please note these wagers are called by different names at the different binary sites, but accomplish the same objective. For example, many sites refer to barrier expiration bets as simply *calls* and *puts*.

Some sites offer additional propositions as well, and attempt to make them sound attractive. I am not fond of any other types of wagers than these. I believe that even if you found a way to get an edge with an exotic bet, you would probably still be better off using one of the above listed wager types instead.

Developing Binary Trading Skills

Trading skills, whether applied to binary options or other forms of trading, mainly consist of chart reading to find entries with a favorable risk vs. reward ratio, and then managing the open positions. Because of the built-in house edge on new positions, we will almost never see an attractive opportunity to sell a bet back early to the binary options broker (only some of them offer this ability, anyway). For the most part, the only trading skill we really need to employ is a little chart reading to help in finding attractive wagers. We only make wagers that we are happy to "die with."

What we are looking for on a chart depends on which trading strategy we are using. But none of the strategies taught in this manual call for more than a basic candlestick chart with a simple indicator or two. No oscillators, no other studies, no spaghetti strewn all over the chart. We just need to see where the price has been recently and what it is doing now. Each strategy has its own particular set-up, but simple charts tell us everything we need to know for all of them.

While chart-reading plays an important part of any trade entry, it is bet pricing that ultimately determines whether or not we have a green light.

Getting the Right Price

Bet pricing is everything at this game. Pick lots of winners but get lousy odds on your plays, and you can easily still come out behind. Bet on more losers than winners but get the right price on your plays, and you will still make money. Playing with the pricing and insisting on only wagering when it is favorable is what successful financial wagering is all about. Unfortunately, the binary options brokers are always changing the pricing around and so there are times when the best bet is not to play, even with a favorable trade set-up. But with so many of them out there nowadays, it does create the opportunity to shop for the best price (and even play arbitrage angles occasionally).

To come out ahead you need to win a high enough percentage of your plays to show a long-run profit based on the average return of each individual bet. For example, if you are betting 10% of your account value on plays that have an average profit of 55% of the amount bet, and your overall winning percentage is 70%, you will show an 8.5% profit for every ten plays. If you could somehow find 20 of these every month you would earn 17% per month on your money. Each bet will have a positive expectation of .85%. On the other hand, winning only 65% of your plays with an average profit of 50% of the amount bet will lose money – each bet will have a negative expectation of -.25% for a total monthly loss of -5% on 20 bets placed. As you can see, your methods are crucial as the line between winning and losing is thin.

Many otherwise playable set-ups will have to be abandoned because your binary site is being stingy with the pricing that day. This can't be avoided. You may find a terrific trade – but if you can't get the right return on your wager, then it is not worth making. "Placing the bet anyway" is what turns so many would-be decent financial bettors into steady losers.

On the other side of the fence, getting good pricing will make a bet playable regardless of what you think of the trade set-up. This is because nobody knows what any financial market will do next, not even you. Consequently, contrarian-type plays are more playable than trend-following plays in short-term "swing" time frames, such as the 5-14 day One-Touch wagers.

To win at binary trading, the total payout of all your winning bets must exceed the total cost of all your losing bets. That may seem obvious, but most binary players don't really think about this – at least, not in the way they need to. It doesn't matter if you are getting even money pricing and are hitting 60%, or you are getting 300% pricing on high-yield plays and are hitting 40% of them. As long as the end result is positive.

Of course, what most players are doing (without even realizing it) is just the opposite. They are doing something like getting 250% pricing but only hitting 30-35% winners, or are getting 85% pricing but are only hitting about half of them. These are both losing operations that will continue to lose unless the win rate vs. bet price becomes positively aligned. The specific strategies discussed in the following pages all have a positive alignment when implemented correctly. The only other element to maximizing our monthly return rate is using an optimal position sizing technique.

Position Sizing for Optimal Returns

This is the money management part of our betting and it is critical to our bottom line. Once we have a winning method of identifying good trade set-ups that are getting the right price, we have to decide how much to bet. If we bet too much, we're assuming an unacceptable risk of blowing our account out (or crippling it) when the inevitable bad string of losses occurs. If we bet too little, we will not make enough of an average monthly return on our account balance for it to be worth our while.

The optimal position size is going to be a certain percentage of our account balance. What percentage depends on the average number of bets the strategy being used is finding every month. This is because if a strategy is not finding more than several bets in a month, more must be risked per wager in order to get a decent amount of capital working for us. Unfortunately, this creates more risk than desired, but it can't be helped. For this reason, a strategy that finds more bets is better. However, there is no winning strategy that I am aware of for beating binary options (other than day-trading the intraday expirations) which makes a lot of bets. If you see someone making bets every day on swing-type trades, I guarantee you they are not winning. Profitable trading set-ups with acceptable pricing just aren't that

The Solutions: How You Can Beat the Game

frequent for expirations ranging from a few days to a few weeks.

The ultimate goal is to achieve a compounding effect so our account balance grows steadily. The best way to do this is to use a position size that is a percentage of our account balance on the first day of the month. This will be our bet size for every wager placed that month, regardless of the outcome of any individual bet. Figure the current value of any open wagers into your account value. For example, if you have $784 in cash and an open wager that the site will buy back for $64 on the first day of March, consider your account balance as being $848. If your position size for the betting strategy you are using is 10% of account balance, then each bet you make in March should be risking about $84.

When making a binary wager, you are choosing a figure that you want to win and then the site tells you how much it will cost. The "amount to win" figures are from a list of available amounts; you have to choose one from their list. So for most wager types, you will have to fool with the pricing a little and just try to get close to your position size number, as you will be unable to nail it exactly.

By the way, 10% is a pretty good position size for most strategies. If you are only placing a few bets per month then 15% may become more optimal, but this is the absolute upper limit. If you are finding say 8-10 plays every month then you might want to use a slightly smaller figure, down to around 7% of account size — which should be the absolute lower limit. Staying within this range will allow you to earn a decent monthly return while keeping the inevitable bad streak from damaging your account too deeply. (Fortunately, good streaks are also inevitable.)

Why You Can Beat the Game

Now that I've given you an outline describing the how of beating the game, let me add some insight as to why it's possible in the first place. I realize I started off by making it seem like it's going to be extremely difficult to do, but I did that in order to get you into the proper mindset. A healthy respect for both the financial markets and the way the binary options sites create an edge for themselves is necessary before you can design a winning game plan.

There are two fundamental reasons why we are able to turn the tables on the binary sites and put the odds in our favor. The first has to do with exploiting inefficiencies in the financial markets which carry through to the wager pricing. The second has to do with our goals for return on capital vs. other trader's goals for return on capital.

Exploiting Market Inefficiencies. The markets themselves present favorable opportunities from time to time for those who know what to look for. One example is the momentum breakout, where the entire market suddenly starts moving in one direction on very heavy trading volume. There is an overwhelming probability for the market to continue in the breakout direction for at least the very short term.

Another example is a new long-term trend in a commodities market that is caused by world economics. This type of trend is almost impossible to reverse and usually continues farther than anyone thinks is possible. Good examples include the price of gold, currency trends, or crude oil.

Probably the best market inefficiencies to exploit are those found in the options markets. Because binaries pricing comes from the options markets, and because many wager types are derived from certain types of options contracts, savvy players can cash in on both overpriced and underpriced option premiums.

The main thing to understand is that when a market is volatile it attracts option buyers hoping to make a big score. This drives up the price of option premiums. When a market is not volatile, just flat-lining along, nobody wants to buy options on it so premiums are cheap. The irony behind this is that a volatile market is more likely to fall into a calm trading range, where a calm, subdued market is more likely to see a sudden big move. Smart options players buy options when volatility is low and sell options when volatility is high. Correspondingly, smart binaries players make One-Touch bets when volatility is low and Range bets when volatility is high. Besides being the only way to get the right pricing on your wagers, it gives you the best chance of winning –

because you are going against the crowd that is always chasing its tail.

Return on Capital Goals. This is another way that losing option buyers help fund our retirement. Option buyers are typically gamblers chasing huge returns. They are looking to double or triple their money on every transaction. We, on the other hand, are happy making a steady 10-15% monthly return on capital. You are happy with that rate of return, aren't you? Because if you aren't, you should probably give it up right now. Even a 7.5% average monthly compounding return will turn a $500 account today with an added $100 monthly deposit into $10,000 in just over two years' time. Not too shabby. If it were reasonably possible to make 25%+ monthly, every knucklehead would be a millionaire and the binary option sites would all be out of business.

It's the fact that most traders are chasing impossible dreams that creates our opportunity. It is extremely difficult to earn more than a 15% average monthly return on capital in any form of trading, including small-time financial betting. However, it's not terribly hard to get on the same philosophical side as the binary options sites and siphon off a nice little monthly return; one that is ultimately paid for by the gamblers who are always trying to double their money while taking the worst of it.

Site Orientation and Wager Type Analysis

If you are new to financial betting, you'll need to take some time to become familiar with the navigation of the binary options sites and pricing out various types of wagers in the different markets. Fortunately, this is pretty straightforward, as the interfaces on most of these sites tend to walk you right through the betting process.

You usually don't need to bother logging in to your account in order to price bets out. I will often price different bets in the markets I am interested in and then login only if I have found one that I want to purchase. The bet pricing menu is easy to find at these sites, but normally only functional during market hours. Typically, you first choose the wager type and then select the market and time frame.

The pricing screen is where you may need to do a little fooling around before you understand it all, but it won't take long. Many have links to a handy little popup window which explains how that type of bet works, and some even have links to live streaming charts of the chosen market. Sometimes, you first need to price out a random bet to get the market correctly showing on the screen, and the default chart to appear.

I refer to using off-site charting in most of the specific strategy chapters in this manual, but many of the binary option brokers do have excellent charting features that you can use right on their site. Nothing wrong with that, either.

After you have priced out a wager you will have the option to purchase it. The offers are, of course, time sensitive.

Your portfolio page is one you will use often, as it shows your account balance and all your open positions.

Some sites have additional tools that are well worth perusing. For example, one I used to trade at had something called a *Price Browser*. This was a spreadsheet format of pricing at different levels for One-Touch, No-Touch, and expiry bets (the primary ones you will be using) for any of the markets from a dropdown menu. That kind of thing can save a lot of time if you know what wagers you want to price out ahead of time and are looking for longer time frames. It also makes a great shopping tool when you want to hunt for pricing anomalies as described in the Price Tracking chapter.

Any volatility charts offered are worth getting familiar with as well. These are a quick way to determine which markets and which types of bets will be priced better than others, as will be touched upon in the

Site Orientation and Wager Type Analysis

Index Straddle & Range chapter. Basically, any market where the volatility is currently high will have attractive Range and No Touch bet pricing, and any market where the volatility is currently low will have attractive Barrier Expiration and One-Touch bet pricing.

Take the newbies' tour and learn about the trade types before sending any site any money. You want to make sure they offer what you need. Pay particular attention to what their "max payout" is. While all sites offer at least some high yield wagers, you want their "standard" max return to be as high as possible, especially if you plan on intraday trading.

Wager Type Analysis

Not all of the wager types offered are worth serious consideration. In fact, some are downright terrible. Much like a smart casino player, you want to avoid the sucker bets. That is, the ones with a large house edge that simply cannot be beaten in the long run, even if you have developed considerable trading skills. Let's look at a few of the more popular wager types.

End of Session Fall/Rise. This is typically an intraday wager that the price of the underlying will be higher or lower than it is now at the close of the current session. It usually must be placed fairly early in the session. A reasonable "commission" is typically added to the current price in the form of a spread hurdle, so you are starting out in a slightly losing position. This is my favorite type of intraday wager, but you need good price and terms. Something like a 90% payout, or maybe a 75% payout with a 15% refund on losers (which is really the same thing).

Shorter Intraday Fall/Rise. An intraday wager that the price of the underlying will be higher or lower at some point during the current market session. Some sites offer these for ridiculously short intervals, such as 60 seconds away. Other options are slightly more reasonable, say two minutes or 5 minutes out. At some sites these can be customized to a wide variety of parameters – for example, by using the standard put/call contracts and simply setting the expiration time before the current market session ends. The problem with all these is, of course, finding decent bet pricing. The shorter time frame bets are designed for gamblers and thus tend to be priced more like sucker bets. In addition, some of them also include a small spread hurdle to insulate the broker even more. All this is because back in the day, sharp day traders learned to beat the straight "double up" intraday wagers that BetonMarkets used to offer. As a result, they no longer exist – anywhere.

Barrier Expiration. You are betting that the price of the underlying will simply be above or below a specified price on a future date (again, some sites simply refer to these as calls and puts). Commissions are figured into the pricing, so this is a pure trading wager – you against the house. With a minimum time frame as early as a few days, this is currently one of the best directional plays available.

Range. You are betting that the price of the underlying will be between two specified prices on a future date. Commissions are figured into the pricing. With a minimum time frame as early as a few days, this is currently one of the best non-directional wagers available.

One-Touch. A wager that the underlying will touch the target price on or before the wager expiration date. Any time the price touches, the wager is over and records as a winner. Commissions are figured into the bet pricing. This is the other directional wager that is worth playing, but the minimum time-frame tends to be longer than on barrier expiration trades.

No Touch. A wager that the underlying will never touch the target price before the expiration date. This one you have to sweat out until the end before you can collect your winnings. In the first edition of this book I advised against these wagers, except for very long terms. However, the pricing on them has improved dramatically over the years, so these bets are now worth a look when devising non-directional strategies. Commissions are included in the bet pricing.

Up or Down. Another barrier-range type play, but with this one you get paid if the price of the underlying touches either barrier. I have not seen pricing on these anywhere near enough to make them attractive, ever – so you should probably just forget about them. A much better alternative is a straddle using two separate One-Touch bets, as described in the Index Straddle & Range chapter.

Spread Bets. Spread bets are a lot like trading real futures contracts. They require margin and will be closed by the broker if they go against you enough to trigger a margin call. You make or lose a set amount for every percentage point the underlying moves in your favor or against you. The commission takes the form of a *spread*, a certain distance the entity must move before you are in the money. These wagers are only available on certain markets and in certain jurisdictions. For that reason, they are not practical to use. Also, the typical 6-pip spread on currencies is a bit high, so you are usually better off using Barrier Expiration, No Touch, or One-Touch bets to accomplish the same objective.

Stop Bets. These are the same thing as the Spread Bets but they require a stop-loss point (which is within the reach of your account equity) instead of using margin. They are also only available in certain markets and jurisdictions, and the commission is the same as with the Spread Bets. Consequently, I don't recommend these, either.

Other Stuff. The binary options sites will occasionally dream up new types of wagers to keep clients interested, in an effort to prevent us from switching to a different site. These are always worth checking out, because sometimes the folks who design them make mathematical mistakes in our favor. You just need to know how to analyze them. Hopefully, the Price Tracking chapter will teach you the necessary skills for doing this.

I'll give you an example here. At one time, the old BetonMarkets site offered something called *Super Doubles*. They paid 4 x the wager on intraday bets and weren't all that hard to hit. Skilled day traders eventually came in and took them to school. No such wager is available today.

Another time, they rolled out a *Publics Orders* page, allowing players to place limit orders and other players to accept them or post their own. In this manner, wagers the site wasn't willing to pay enough on had a chance to find a taker among all the other traders. BetonMarkets simply matched the wagers and took a small fee for themselves. I used to kill these things, finding suckers that would take badly-priced wagers on the less popular currency pairs. But alas, we begin to leave the arena of fixed odds financial betting and get more into a betting exchange atmosphere with this kind of thing.

Conclusion

When you first open your binary options accounts, it's going to be tempting to jump in and start playing and making different kinds of wagers. They have it set up so it's fun. That's cool and all, and you probably should make a few small newbie bets just to get a feel for things. But not many. Keep your initial bets small and get the new toy fascination out of your system as quickly as you can. I'm actually hoping you lose those first few bets so you'll settle down. Time to get serious.

Directional and Non-Directional Trading Tactics

Most trading strategies based on technical analysis (chart-reading) can be divided into two general categories: *Trend Following* or *Range Trading*. Range trading is also known as reversal or classic swing trading. So basically, you are either attempting to ride a trend or you are betting against the continuation of recent price move. Either of these approaches can be traded directionally or non-directionally.

Directional trading means you need the price of the underlying entity (stock, index, currency pair, commodity, whatever) to move a certain distance in a defined direction in order to profit.

Non-directional trading tactics are less popular and involve the use of derivatives (futures and/or options contracts of one type or another). This strategy usually bets against one direction only, but sometimes bets against both directions and needs a tight sideways pattern in order to profit. Usually, its only ally is time, attempting to capture an options premium.

As a binary options trader, you can employ both directional and non-directional tactics. You have a great variety of wagering instruments at your disposal and can be quite creative in the way you open and manage your positions, much like a derivatives trader. There is almost nothing that some big-shot Wall Street or Chicago professional trader can do that you cannot effectively emulate in the stock, index futures, gold, or currencies markets.

Here is a beautiful example of a trend:

This is a candlestick-style chart. Starting in July of 2006, the New Zealand dollar began a solid uptrend. Notice the stair-climbing pattern that is typical of trends, making higher highs and lower lows. This is the sort of thing that trend-traders want to bet on. The usual strategy is to wait until one of those not-lower lows completes (bounces up a little), then enter a long position. Exiting the trade is a bit trickier. Some traders will wait until the trend is broken, meaning that the price drops below a previous low – that is, below one of the previous steps on the staircase. Those with a shorter-term outlook might get out when a new high is made, especially if it appears to be running out of steam, and then repeat the process after the next low prints (as long as the trend is not broken).

Many traders are fond of putting statistical studies all over their charts. There are so many of these available nowadays that you wouldn't see the price action anymore if you used more than just a few of them. One of the most useful for trend-following is a price channel, which can be inserted as a study or drawn on manually, like this.

Price channels are useful when wanting to play the swings within a trend. Trend-following means you only enter trades in the direction of the current trend. So you would only be interested in long positions on this chart, and would look for them when the price bounces off the bottom channel. The position would be exited for a profit when the price approaches the upper channel, or closed for a loss if it moved lower outside the channel (which would break the trend).

To draw price channels on your charts, just connect two lows and place the upper channel along one or more highs. Do the opposite for downtrends.

The problem with trends is they look great after the fact but by the time you recognize them, it is getting a bit late to join the party. In July or August the above NZD trend would not have jumped off the chart like it does now. In fact, it would have been considered to be in a trading range by most technicians. But some trends do continue for a very long time, and many believe the odds are always a little more in your favor when you are trading in the direction of a trend in a higher time frame.

Range trading tactics are called for during range-bound markets. Here is an example.

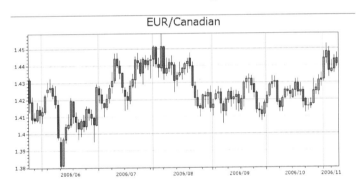

As you can see, price is contained between the high 1.30's and the mid 1.40's on this currency pair. As a range trader, you simply enter a position when the price is near either of these extremes. A great example is at the hard right edge of this chart – that is, where price is currently trading. This is a perfect place to enter a short position, or a wager that the price will move back into the middle of the range from here. Note that this can also be accomplished via a non-directional trade by simply betting the price will **not** go to 1.46 or 1.47.

When price breaks through a trading range, that action is known as a *breakout*. If it continues directionally from there, then that establishes a new trend and the trend followers move in. If it falls back into the previous range instead, it is considered a false breakout and the range traders take over again. If price just trades sideways after a breakout, then that would be a new range, and if it then breaks back down into the previous range that would just expand the chart into a larger range (this is what happened on the EUR/Canadian chart above).

It's all relative to your trading time-frame, of course. If you screw down to a smaller time-frame, you will have a completely different charting landscape. For example, look at the hard right edge of EUR/Canadian daily chart above. If you were to call up an hourly chart on this currency pair, it would show as a solid uptrend.

Breakouts often pull back to the edge of the previous range and test that level. Before the breakout that edge was called resistance; after the breakout that edge is called support. If support holds and the price bounces back up from it, then that is considered the beginning of a new trend. Playing break-outs is very popular because it gets you on board a new trend at the beginning, and who knows how far it can go. Aggressive traders will enter on the break itself, while more conservative traders will wait for a pullback to bounce before getting on board (which may or may not actually happen).

You can see where the range broke into a trend on our NZD chart quite easily when we draw a line across the resistance area:

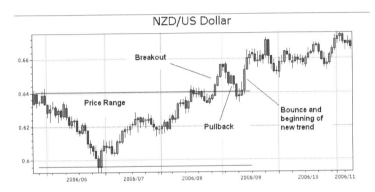

This now begins to look like a more easily tradable scenario than the first time we glanced at this chart. As price first approached the top of the price range and stalled back, the range trader would have gone short – and lost in this instance, as price turned up again and broke through resistance. This is not a great example of a range, as it was only the first test of the upper boundary so it had not been firmly established yet. It's better to trade more clearly defined ranges.

The aggressive breakout trader would have been sweating that first pullback after the breakout. It was severe, breaching the previous range a little, which is actually quite common. The more conservative breakout trader waiting for the bounce would have had a much easier time of it. I personally prefer taking the more conservative route when playing breakouts on the daily chart.

And so you will see this scenario play out on chart after chart in all different time-frames across all markets. Range traders and breakout traders meet at the range extreme to battle it out. One group wins and the other moves on to new charts. When the breakout succeeds, it attracts trend-followers. This is the charting landscape of every financial market in the world.

Trading with Binary Options

As a binary options trader, you will not be buying or selling stocks, index futures, options, option spreads, or currency pair positions. You will be placing outright bets on the underlying entities instead. Using the different types of wagers that were discussed in the last chapter, you will accomplish the same task of taking various positions on different sides of ranges, trends, and breakouts as your strategy dictates.

The biggest difference between you and a broker-based trader is that you will not be so concerned with stop-loss points and profit-taking levels. These risk control measures that broker-based traders must employ are automatically accounted for in your binaries wagering by your bet pricing and position-sizing. But what you are doing is essentially the same thing. That's why it's ridiculous that certain types of binary options are not allowed in some countries, when these same countries allow derivatives-trading that accomplishes the exact same position only with more risk!

It is my goal to train you to be a winning trader who happens to use binary options, not to be a binaries player that understands trading concepts. There is a big difference in my mind, which will become plainly evident when you eventually make the leap from financial betting to broker-based trading.

Understanding Market Liquidity

A winning trader understands the relationship between trading volume, bid and ask spreads, and price movement. This in turn dictates which setups are worth pursuing. You are going to be placing bets on or against price movements largely based on what price has recently done. It is necessary to discern the difference between prior price moves that were significant and ones that were not. Insignificant price movements are often referred to by traders as *noise*.

At the binary options site you aren't worried about having liquid markets to trade in, because they will always take your bet and really there are no exit strategies – you live or die with the result. But in the real world you need to pay strict attention to market liquidity and avoid illiquid markets such as thinly-traded stocks. They aren't worth messing with, because you can get burned too easily by a dishonest market and are paying too much in "commissions" to open your position in the first place. This is especially true with low-volume option contracts, and also currency dealers who charge a wide pip spread on some of the less popular pairs. So stick with high-volume, small bid-ask spread trading vehicles when trading at the brokers.

But there is another important concept involving liquidity as well. It has to do with volume and price movement. Any price move that occurred on low volume cannot be trusted, period. Breakouts that print on low volume spikes don't mean that much, and will likely fail. In fact, fading (betting against) low-volume breakouts is a very viable trading strategy.

Most trading volume occurs during certain peak market hours and it's the moves during those times that count. Lunchtime at the NYSE typically sees anemic volume, so mid-session movement on the indices is usually all noise and can safely be ignored – most of the time. But when something significant does happen during off-times, it will be accompanied by a sharp increase in volume.

For this reason, afterhours market trading is better suited for range-trading than finding breakouts. However, trend followers can often get the pullback bounce they are looking for during off-hours. Currency traders really need to pay attention to this! Forex is advertised as this wonderful 24-hour trading market and there is some truth in that, but if you are making directional plays then you had better be trading during the high-volume hours – namely, the London/New York overlap period from 8:00 am to noon EST. If you are day trading it during any other hours, you best stick to range-trading tactics.

Here is an example:

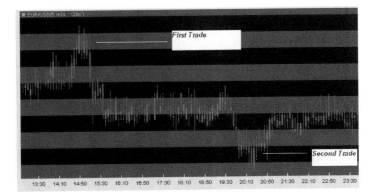

What you want to do afterhours in the currencies is to fade the moves. Bet against breakouts, extended moves, and range-extremes, as there just isn't enough volume to carry them much farther. This can be accomplished using binaries by playing the end-of-session contracts, or possibly even something a little shorter. On the example above, there were two good after-hours plays that could have been made on the EUR/USD, which both would have won. This is my preferred method of making intraday Forex wagers.

Conclusion

By now you should have a firm grasp of the financial markets charting landscape, and the typical trading tactics that accompany it. Some excellent advice was smuggled into this chapter that will make for great trading strategies in the right mindset. In the following chapters, at least five more specific trading strategies will be discussed at length – with a few more good ones thrown in via a quick paragraph here and there.

Whether you realize it or not, you are quickly becoming armed with the proper psychology for trading success. My guess is you are also already forming certain ideas into some of your own personal strategies. Temper any excitement over newfound knowledge with the patience and discipline that is stressed throughout this manual. Using your ammunition properly will win battles and, ultimately, the war. But misusing it can result in having it explode in your face.

Beat Binary Options

Choosing a Market and Strategy

You probably won't be able to work all of the strategies described in this book. Even if you can, you probably shouldn't. Most successful traders learn to do one or two things well, in one or two markets, and concentrate their efforts accordingly. Specializing is a winning attribute. Trying to do everything in all markets will make you scatterbrained. Worse, it may lessen your propensity to develop the sixth sense that traders who specialize in one market using one or two strategies often come to rely upon.

On the other hand, there's no reason you can't operate two or three of these strategies profitably, especially if you become an expert in one particular market. The markets you decide to specialize in will likely be the ones that appeal to you for one reason or another. Very often, they are decided by time frames. If you don't have time to mess with the stock market during trading hours, then currencies may be your thing.

Each market available for wagering at the binary options sites exhibits certain unique features. Let's look at those now.

Indices: Very erratic in the short term most of the time, but display some very reliable break-out patterns on occasion. Dependable long-term trends do develop, but it can be years between them. Short-term break-outs, short-term range-bound reversals, long-term trends, and medium-term changes in volatility make the best betting set-ups.

Individual Stocks: Reliable short-term trends certainly develop, but just as often stocks will trade inside a range – sometimes a predictable one. Congestion patterns are more common, though. Fundamentals such as earnings expectations can occasionally be used to make plays. Medium-term changes in volatility, long-term trend riding, and short-term trend reversals are usually the best bets.

Commodities: Display very reliable long-term trends when they develop, but are typically characterized by many sharp corrections along the way. Short-term trend reversals and long term trend plays are the only practical bets in these markets.

Currencies: Both short-term and long-term trends tend to be reliable, especially when a new one is first confirmed. Short-term break-outs in currencies are less reliable than those that occur with the indices, but ones that jump out of a long basing pattern can be profitably played. This is a very popular market, and one that offers flexible trading hours. However, a trader must be aware that break-outs only really work during the 4-hour overlap period between London and New York. One-Touch bets and intraday fall/rise bets are the way to play currencies.

Those are the markets. Now let's get a quick description of our trading strategies.

1. The Intraday Break-out. Playable on indices and currencies. The trader must be available to watch the market closely during the entire market day. For currency traders, this really means being available for the 4-hour London/New York overlap. Afterhours breakouts are significantly less reliable and are even worth fading. Index traders just need to be available during stock market hours for whichever continent you are trading. The wager of choice is the intraday rise/fall bet, or a call/put with a specified in-session target that is getting good odds.

The intraday break-out strategy requires the most attention to the market and the most patience of any of my trading strategies. For this reason, it will be impractical for a lot of folks. Many who try it will become too bored or too distracted to trade it correctly. And no wonder – for all of your constant attention to the market there is only an average of about 3-4 plays per month (per market). Less than 1 per week! Most of you reading this manual will be very surprised that a day trading strategy would have so few trade entries. Hey, I wish there were more, and on some months there will be. But if you want to win you will have to wait for the real momentum breakouts and there just aren't that many.

Your patience will be rewarded with a high win ratio; somewhere around 75% of your bets will win. Consequently, this is an extremely profitable strategy. But because it is so demanding on your attention, only those with a true passion for following the daily movements of the financial markets are likely to succeed with it.

2. Big Picture Positioning. On the complete opposite end of the spectrum from the intraday breakout, this strategy is best applied to currencies and commodities, especially gold and oil. Bets are made for the long term and typically have very low returns on the amount wagered. But they are still profitable, as they almost never lose (when done correctly). This is a hands-off approach that can be played by anyone. You should add it as a supplement to whatever other strategies you want to specialize in, as it does not generate enough returns to be worthwhile by itself. The wager being used is the No-Touch bet, typically for long time-frames.

It takes a while for the bet results to be realized, and sometimes selling them back early for a small profit (where allowed) is the best way to close the position. A quick glance at the market once or twice a month is all that is required to follow and manage the trade. Entries are usually discovered simply by following the news in the financial markets and then pulling up long-term charts. Two or three good trade set-ups per year is about average. If this is the only strategy you use then you will not be actively trading enough to build wealth aggressively – but it is still worthwhile having a binary options account to take advantage of these opportunities.

3. One-Touch Reversal. This tactic works best on indices and currencies. Short-term market trends are tracked. The trader should be looking for (and following) attractive markets on an almost daily basis, waiting for the right set-up to present itself. The market tracking can be done at any time of day, but the bets themselves will have to be placed during market hours, preferably towards the end of the session. The wager used is the One-Touch bet.

Because this is a contrarian's approach to the market, the trader must have the heart to wager in the opposite direction of the short-term trend. Bets are made for the short to medium-term time frame. This is a very satisfying system to trade profitably. It is appealing to many because it doesn't require a whole lot in the way of research to find entries, and the wagers conclude relatively quickly.

A little more than one-third of your bets will win, just enough to squeak out a decent return on capital. You will find 3-5 decent plays (per market) in a typical month. This is a highly-professional betting strategy that benefits from a strict, disciplined approach to finding trade set-ups and an insistence upon getting the right price.

4. Index Straddle & Range-Bet. Here is a professional options trading approach that bets on changes in volatility. It works best on the most volatile trading vehicle, which is very often the NASDAQ or DAX index. Bets are made for the shortest term possible, which is usually a 4-6 trading day period. All the research for trade setups can be done after hours, but it is beneficial to be able to access your account at several times during the market day to try and finagle the best pricing. The bets used are either a One-Touch or a Range.

This is a great strategy for traders who like to follow stock market trends in all time frames. It's another contrarian approach, betting against current extreme market conditions immediately continuing. These wagers can be a lot of fun to put on, so it makes for an exciting betting system. Expect to find only 2-3 wagers per month (per market) but that's plenty. The win ratio will be between 50% and 60%, but the wagers pay god odds. This one is best suited for those who love the stock market and can envision themselves one day becoming a professional trader.

5. Price Tracking for Value. Picture yourself as Warren Buffet or Peter Lynch searching for value-investing opportunities, but on an extremely miniaturized scale. Only it's not the company you are interested in, it's the return you can get on your bet. And it's not just stocks – you are content to hunt for value bets on any contract the binary option broker offers, over any term that you can get a deal on.

If you are a natural born bargain hunter, this strategy will fit you like a glove. It does take some work to pursue, and most of it must be done during market hours. Every day you will need to price out a series of bets that you are tracking prices on. You will be rewarded for your efforts with several plays every month that stand out like a sore thumb; bets that will swing the advantage to your side. These will be randomly-occurring directional plays so the results will be streaky, but in the long run you will show a nice profit from them. This strategy integrates well with any of the other four if you have the time for it.

Which Strategies?

This is probably a silly question for me to try and help you with, because by now you most likely have already decided which ones are for you. That's great, because designing a trading plan that suits your situation and personality is probably the single most important thing you can do. Don't try to trade a market and strategy that just doesn't fit your interests and/or schedule no matter how much you think that is the way to make money. For you, right now at least, it isn't. Successful trading isn't so much about using the most profitable strategies as it is working a plan that integrates into your life well.

Everyone should use strategy #2, because that's just gravy. What you decide your core strategy(s) will be is much more subject to personal fit. Certain ones go together well just based on the type of research involved, and the optimal mentality for locating good entries. For example, Strategies #3 and #4 are very similar in nature and time-frames, so they are a natural for the average person with a full time job (that can get online for personal purposes during market hours). Strategies #1 and #5 may be perfect for someone who obsesses over the stock market daily and is looking for a way to capitalize on their observations.

Keep in mind that you really don't need to use more than one core strategy to be successful. In fact, choosing just one to focus on could be what tilts the odds enough in your favor for you to reach optimal performance. Always remember: It's the average monthly return on capital that's important, not the number of bets you make or the amount of market research you are doing.

Strategy #1: Mastering the Intraday Breakout

Day trading does not necessarily mean making a lot of trades. It does, however, mean paying constant attention to intraday market movements and always being ready to jump on the obvious opportunities when they present themselves. In fact, staying away from all the mediocre setups and only moving on the occasional blatant signal that is screaming to be entered is an extremely high-odds approach. That's exactly what this strategy is all about. Your continuous monitoring of the market during trading hours will be rewarded with wagering opportunities that are overwhelming favorites to win.

But you have to stay away from everything else! What good will it do to get a 75% win rate on these wagers if you are frivolously blowing all the winnings on less than premium trade setups? Take the time to realize the logic behind this trading strategy. Let it sink in until you understand at a deep level why it works. Any intraday bet that you make which does not meet the trade setup requirements is simply gambling with the odds against you. Every time you do this you will be sabotaging your results.

It's completely understandable why you might want to make additional bets. Following this strategy correctly will only produce 2-3 wagers per month on average (betting the indices). In order to get these few signals you have to watch the stock market – all day, every day. So there may be times when you are tempted to bet simply because you get a "feeling" that the market is headed higher or lower that day. Don't do it. If you had a nickel for every trading account that was blown out because people abandoned their trading rules to act on a feeling, you would have no need to trade.

Please note that the instructions for this strategy are written specifically for playing the indices. Forex bettors looking to play an intraday breakout strategy should read the entire chapter and then pay special attention to the Currency Betting section towards the end.

Following these rules will keep you in very high-odds wagers.

Tools

Charting. You need access to streaming intraday charts to work this strategy (streaming means they are tracking current live prices as they move, without having to refresh the chart). Many of the binary options sites offer free ones. If yours doesn't, use one of the following solutions.

Fortunately, there are free streaming charts available on the internet if you don't mind being bothered with advertisements and/or email solicitations to open a brokerage account. Search for *free streaming charts* and you will have a half-dozen or so choices from places like FreeStockCharts.com, Quotetracker.com, etc.

Another option is the free streaming chart service from Scottrade located at www.scottrader.com. With that one you only have to put up with occasional Scottrade solicitations to open an account with them. (Which, by the way, isn't a bad idea if you are looking for a U.S.-based broker. I am extremely pleased with my Scottrade account. Great executions and rock-bottom commissions.)

You could open a broker account to get access to live quotes and streaming charts. Most online brokers will let you open an account with as little as $500. This may not be a practical option if you are starting on a shoestring budget.

Time Frames. Use a **15-minute chart** for this strategy. The signals are clearest with about a 4-day look-back period. In other words, use a 4-day 15-minute chart, or something close to that.

Chart Type. If you prefer bar charts you are certainly free to use them, but I highly recommend switching to candlesticks. They just seem to give a clearer signal, being either solid red or solid green and expanding rapidly out of the recent trading range. Forget about using a line chart.

Indicators & Oscillators. Just volume, baby. Forget about the rest. They aren't needed, and tend to obscure the picture rather than enhance it. Oh, all right, if you insist you can throw a moving average on the chart as a reference point – just one, though! And I guess it won't hurt to put some kind of oscillator under the volume window, such as the Slow Stochastics, as long as you don't pay any attention to it. A breakout system doesn't look for confirmation from these types of things – if the price starts breaking out of a clearly-defined range fast on heavy volume we get on board, pronto.

There is one indicator that is not chart-based which I like to have handy, and that is the *Trin*. This is a measure of up volume vs. down volume on the NYSE and it gives a good picture of the overall flavor of the market on any given day. A reading of 90 is about neutral, large sell-off days will have readings much higher and big rally days will have readings much lower. Please note this indicator is much handier for trend trading than breakouts. I always have it showing as a separate 3-minute line chart over about a 4-hour period. I look to see if it is spiking in one direction or another when there is a close decision to be made on a breakout. It's not necessary for working this strategy, but you might like to have it up as a reference for what's going on in the market – being as most days you won't be making any plays.

Tickers. This intraday betting strategy can almost be worked without using a chart at all if you become adept at just watching the tickers for the major

Strategy #1: Mastering the Intraday Breakout

indices. When they all start moving suddenly in one direction it's time to perk up and pay attention. What you are missing in order to make a trading decision is, of course, a volume indicator. So the best way to use tickers is as an alert that tells you to quickly check your chart. Usually this is because you have minimized your chart and are working on something else. Keeping a stock index ticker in the corner of your screen, or having CNBC (or Bloomberg) on a nearby television that you can keep glancing over at, is all you really need to keep abreast of what's happening.

What to Chart & What to Trade

The major stock indices are all chartable themselves, but there's one problem. The sudden surge in trading volume that is critical to our entry signal will often be very subtle and easy to miss on a 15-minute chart. No bueno. We need a clear-cut, screaming signal from the volume indicator before placing a wager.

There are plenty of tradable entities representing various market indices that we can chart as an alternative. The best one for our purposes is SPY, commonly known as the S&P spider, which is the ETF (exchange traded fund) for the S&P 500. Not just because it includes the most stocks, making it the broadest market index, but also because it trades a large daily volume. When SPY starts moving on a volume spike it's a very good indication that the entire market is breaking. The other ETF's representing the betable U.S. indices include DIA (Diamonds) and QQQ (Cubes), which are also good chartable entities that give reliable volume signals. It's best to use SPY as our standard chart and then check both DIA and QQQ for confirmation on our entry signals.

So SPY is what you chart, but which index do you place your bet on? This is a more difficult question to answer because things are always changing in the markets and also with bet pricing at the binary options sites. The short answer would be that it doesn't matter – and in reality, it doesn't. We're betting on entire market moves, so the winning percentages should be about equal overall. But there may be a way to increase your edge by figuring out which bet has the cheapest commission (best pricing and/or smallest initial spread hurdle) relative to the average daily price move. Those of you who are good with statistics might be able to piece this puzzle together.

Personally, I have had the best luck with the Dow (in the U.S. market), so that's what I usually bet. There is one additional consideration, however. Sometimes the S&P and Dow will break first before the NASDAQ finally joins the party. This can cause us to delay in making our bet, as anything other than a broad-based move is subject to sputter and reverse. But if the other two are really taking off, the NASDAQ will have no choice but to eventually follow – and when it finally throws in the towel and starts moving, it will have a lot of catching up to do. So in this instance the NASDAQ is the best bet, especially if you are a little late getting on board.

Strategy #1: Mastering the Intraday Breakout

OK – you have your streaming 15-minute chart of the SPY set up, and your binary options account opened and funded. Now it's time to watch and wait for the set-up to appear.

When to Trade

The first hour of the trading day is not playable. Don't even think about it. (This may be good news if you live on the U.S. west coast and don't want to get up that early anyway.) The market-watching day for this strategy in the U.S. markets starts at 10:30 a.m. EST, or whenever the first hour of trading is complete for the other markets. The first hour establishes an important trading range which acts as a reference point for the rest of the day. Sometimes the first hour is completely directional, but usually not. Sometimes the break we are looking for shoots out of the established first hour range, where it picks up momentum from all the first hour range-breakout traders. Other times, the market is trading sideways outside of the first hour range when it breaks for us, in either direction.

The middle of the trading day is usually not playable, either. At the time of this writing that would be between 12:00 and 1:00 EST when many NYSE traders are at lunch. If market hours get expanded this could change, but basically Wall Street likes to go to lunch – and without them, we normally can't get the volume we need for a breakout. There are exceptions from time to time, but they're relatively rare. Most breakouts during lunch hour fail, even if they're getting what seems like a volume spike at the time. There needs to be a real fundamental reason behind a lunch hour break for it to continue – like breaking major news or a political event.

Some binary options sites do not allow intraday bets during the last ninety minutes of the trading day, which is after 2:30 p.m. EST. That leaves us with 1 1/2 hours in the morning and 1 1/2 hours in the afternoon. So you are not actually watching the entire market day looking for bets. It's those specific three hours that present our trading opportunities. But it really helps get you in tune with the market if you are watching it all day long, every day. Being in tune with the market trains you to just sort of "know" when market conditions are ripe for a breakout. It's a skill you develop by keeping a constant eye on the stock market. Those that love the market, that have a real passion for it, are better equipped and better prepared for the breakouts when they occur. Probably more importantly, they are better at sniffing out the false breakouts and staying off the sucker rallies.

That being said, I live in California myself and just don't get up early enough to watch the first hour. This is no handicap, as when I first log on I can see exactly what has happened thus far and get an instant flavor for the type of market day that is likely in store. Breakouts do not take me by surprise very often these days.

Strategy #1: Mastering the Intraday Breakout

Trade Preparation

The first thing you need to do every day when you sit down at your computer is log on to your binary options trading account and locate the intraday wager pricing field. Make sure you have indices selected as your market. Know what your wager size is so you are ready to go in a moment's notice. You can't make any trades unless you are logged on and know the plan. This is an extremely important part of your morning ritual – resist the temptation to check out the market first, as it is just too easy to get distracted. When a bet signal does occur, you will be at a serious disadvantage if you then have to go to the binaries site, log on, and get to the right betting screen. By that time, the market may have moved enough to make a further move covering the commission spread a close to even-money proposition. This betting strategy does not operate on close to even-money propositions. It bets on high-odds continuations of what looks to be a major intraday movement developing, and timing the bet is crucial to your success. Don't get caught with your binaries screen down.

The bet you will be making depends on the site you are using, but always find the highest payout you can. The binary options sites are always changing things. Unfortunately, many of them have capped intraday payouts at levels like 80%. At the time of this writing, there is one decent site (that accepts U.S. players) offering 95% payouts on intraday plays. That's where I would play. Another site offering 85% payouts with a 10% refund if you lose accomplishes the same thing.

Alternatively, some of the sites let you price out intraday wagers on their standard put/call contracts, which works well – especially if you can finagle 100% or better pricing. Things are always changing and the marketplace is competitive, so do keep abreast of what the different sites are offering and investigate special "new" types of intraday propositions that are rolled out to see if they fit your purpose.

I am partial to end-of-session contracts, or time frames that are at least one hour out. However, it is certainly possible to adopt this system to a shorter time frame such as 15 minutes. Just be aware that there are usually short pullback periods even on the most directionally-continuing breakout days that could make your position a loser even if you correctly call the breakout. Those may, however, wash out evenly in the long run. Give yourself at least an hour and you should win 100% of your correctly-called breakouts.

If you are going to minimize your chart during premium trading hours, make sure you have a stock market ticker within an easy glance – either in the corner of your computer screen or on a nearby television.

The overwhelming majority of the time you are watching the market it will be unexciting. Sideways movement and drifting slowly higher or lower are the usual tendencies. A good day trader with a brokerage account can capitalize on intraday trends, but a binary options player usually cannot. This is because intraday trends are not reliable enough to play profitably against fixed-odds commission structures (the skewed bet pricing and/or initial spread hurdle). A day trader with a brokerage account has the luxury of seeing when a market trend is flattening out or reversing and then exiting the trade. Intraday binaries players do not. Once the wager is made, you must live or die with the results. Trust me; these binary option sites make their living from players who think they can ride intra-day trends. Please don't be one of them.

Our bets are made when something strikingly out of the ordinary takes place. We act upon a sudden call to action. It's like a wake-up call or a fire alarm going off. Our trade setups are obvious. In fact, that's the easiest way to describe them: obvious. We make a bet only when it is ridiculously obvious, when it is screaming to be made. This keeps us away from all the gambling situations and only puts us in high-odds propositions. The discipline to do this is what makes us winning players. The lack of discipline to do this will sabotage the best of intentions and ultimately leave our accounts shipwrecked on the rocks (alongside nearly everyone else's).

The Setup

Allrighty then – you have your 15-minute streaming chart set up to track the SPY and you have your binary options account open and minimized at the ready. You are watching the market all day long and are getting a good feel for it on a day-to-day basis. When are you supposed to make a bet?

If you have followed the instructions so far, the rest is going to be easy. The most difficult thing, as already mentioned, is laying off the trigger finger and being content to wait for the relatively few obvious signals that occur. The profitable betting signals are so blatant you probably don't need to read any further in order to recognize them. They simply jump off the chart and shout at you. If you are watching the market, and are good at sitting on your hands, then you will have a birds-eye view when something out of synch starts happening.

Many traders will be panicking when the signal occurs, but this is your opportunity. Because you have no position yet, because you are on the sidelines, you can take advantage of these adverse moves. Here then, is your trade setup checklist:

1. A candle (or bar) is expanding rapidly out of the recent SPY trading range

2. A volume bar significantly larger than the recent volume bars is spiking up fast

3. Condition #1 and #2 are both also happening on symbol DIA and QQQ

4. All three index tickers are suddenly moving fast in the same direction

That's it. There's your signal. You'd think it would happen more often than in actually does. Some months it will. Some months, however, there will be no signals at all. But there are enough over the course

Strategy #1: Mastering the Intraday Breakout

of a year to more than double your account balance by sticking with this system. And a 100%+ annual return is enough to become wealthy over the next decade, even starting with a small account size.

The most important part of the setup is the volume spike. Without it, you don't have a play. Markets that start moving without volume invariably sputter and die. We only want to bet on real intraday sudden movements, ones that have the legs to carry them quite a bit further.

That's why we cross-check the other two ETF's for confirmation. That's also why we use the SPY as the primary charting entity. And it's also why we use a 15 minute chart – volume spikes on a 5-minute chart are not sustained enough to give a reliable signal. By the time you get price movement and volume spiking on a 15-minute chart, you really might have something. Trying to trade this strategy using only a 5-minute chart will lead to early entries and too many losing bets. A bit of patience and confirmation by using 15-minute charts on all three indices goes a long way towards confirming the break.

Timing Your Entry

While early entries are a problem, so are late ones. If several expansion bars have already taken place on a 15-minute chart and you are just noticing it now because you were sleeping, you missed the move so forget about it. The trick to winning with this system is timing. You must avoid jumping the gun and strike a balance between a good early entry and waiting for solid confirmation that the market is really breaking. If you are going to error it's better to error on the late side, as early entries are a far worse hazard than slightly late ones. However, by "slightly late" I am talking about early in the second 15-minute bar. Any bet made later than that becomes progressively less likely to win. Notice that the signal checklist above describes your entry point as being on the first bar of the move. The optimal point, in my experience, is during the latter half of that bar. Right when it becomes obvious that the one developing before your eyes is probably going to end solid and completely enclosed.

Where it gets tricky is on a volume spike that is large but not huge. If it is the largest bar that has printed in the last couple of days, and it has yet to complete, it is probably playable. Keep in mind that volume bars are higher just before and just after lunch than during lunch. Likewise, they are higher at both the beginning of the day and at the end of the day than at all points in between. They start big, get progressively smaller towards the middle of the day, and then get progressively bigger again towards the end of the day. It is a deviation from this normal pattern that you are concerned with catching.

Of course, price movement also has to be there! Rogue volume spikes will print from time to time with no real price breakout to speak of. Volume spikes are a confirming indicator, not the primary signal. Always watch price first and volume second. When you see

Strategy #1: Mastering the Intraday Breakout

SPY start moving suddenly away from the recent trading area, look at the volume. If it is spiking, switch the chart over to DIA. If both conditions are present there, call up QQQ. If price and volume are both spiking there as well, go back to SPY again and take another look. The price bar should be much larger than all the recent bars by now and growing. Check the prices of the indices on the ticker - are they all moving rapidly? Yes? Make the bet.

Hold off on the bet if any of the above corresponding conditions you are seeking are not up to speed. The market does have false breakouts, and you need to be careful not to bet into one. Any stalling or hesitation of the initial break is plenty of reason to stop dead in your tracks. Just wait a bit and see if this thing really has legs. It can be frustrating to do this, because sometimes you end up staying off a winner. This typically happens when the market drifts directionally the rest of the day. Just remember that betting on intraday trends is a losing proposition at binary option sites. We need a high-odds play – a sudden, screaming market break showing no signs of weakness that we can get on as soon as it becomes obvious and confirmable.

Here is a chart from a week that had one – well, maybe two – playable setups. Both bets would have won, but the first signal was a bit hazy, having somewhat less than a majestic volume spike. A slightly late entry probably would have been the only way to play it, after seeing where the volume bar ended. Don't worry if you miss a few marginal plays like this, as these are the type that most of your losses will come from. The second signal two days later, however, was the type you just can't miss. Notice how much more obvious it was, how the volume spike was way out of the normal pattern, and how much easier this bet was to make before the 15-minute price and volume bars ended. Your timing would have probably had you in several minutes before the first breakout bar ended, which is optimal.

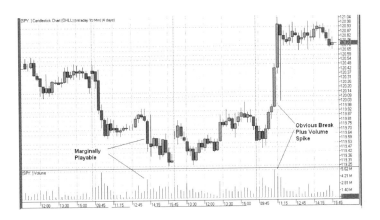

This is the classic breakout signal - the one you will be making all your profits from. Take a good look. Get familiar with it. Embrace it, learn to love it. Look for it every day, but don't ever attempt to will it to happen or you might start seeing it develop when it just isn't there. A detached, unemotional observation will allow you to catch it when it actually happens and avoid putting your money on wishes, dreams, and hopes.

Position Sizing

Because the trade setups occur relatively infrequently, and because there is such a high win rate on these wagers, your position size for this system should be at the upper end of the allowable scale. Since the maximum on that scale is 15%, I recommend betting 12% to 15% of your account balance on each play. That's 12-15% risked, not to win. For simplicity purposes, and for achieving a monthly compounding effect, choose your bet size at the beginning of each month and make the same size wager for each and every play which materializes that month.

For example: If at the beginning of May you have $435 in your account, your optimal per-bet risk size is about $65. That would be to win back about $123, which is about $58 profit. In other words, risk $65 to win $58. (This is why it's critical to have a 70%+ win rate, and why you need to shop for the best pricing among the reputable binary options sites.)

Statistically, what should happen is you will make 3 bets in May. Two will win and one will lose, for a profit of $51 or 12% on your account balance. Starting in June, you will have a $500 account. So, 15% of that is $75, so every bet you make in June will be to win $67. Every month your account and bet size will grow. This is how you can build up a big account, one month at a time. Those who are in more of a hurry to become rich are the ones keeping the binary options sites in business.

Currency Betting

The forex market lends itself extremely well to day trading. However, this is mostly due to the reliability of short-term trends in currency pairs, and not so much due to the reliability of intraday breakouts. Consequently, the intraday breakout system taught in this course will have a lower winning percentage when adapted to the forex betting menu. It should still be over 55% and thus profitable, however, and the lower win rate can at least be partially offset by the increased frequency of trades.

The primary problem is that there is no volume indicator, so we don't have the glaring signal that the entire market is moving like we do on the stock indices. Even if we had a volume indicator, it wouldn't do much good – as there is just too much volume constantly traded in the spot currency market.

There are two things we can do to try and make up for this handicap. The first is to pay particular attention to the actual price patterns before the breakout and stick to the ones that show the highest degree of reliability (as far as a continued move after the breakout goes). The second is to only play when the highest volume is trading, which means avoiding the market during those times when either London or New York are closed.

The price pattern you want to be watching for is a breakout from a consolidation trading range – the tighter, longer, and more definable that range is, the

Strategy #1: Mastering the Intraday Breakout

better. The breakout should take place on a much larger size bar than any that have printed inside the trading range. Do not bet on breakouts from trading ranges that are only a few bars long. The pattern should take up nearly a third of your chart or more before you can really define it as a range.

Five minute charts work best for intraday forex charting. The free streaming charts available at FXCM, a reputable forex broker, work great for finding trade setups.

The best pair to bet on is usually EUR/USD, but USD/YEN, USD/GBP, and EUR/YEN are also good tradable pairs that display playable moves. I highly recommend **picking just one** and concentrating on that alone. All the major currency pairs are correlated to a degree, so trying to follow more than one is probably not going to generate any more profits than just following one of the majors.

Our betting signal occurs on the second expansion bar out of the trading range. Both need to be directional, one almost on top of the other, and both must be larger than all (or nearly all) of the bar sizes in the recent trading range. This is the break we look for. Here is an example.

Beat Binary Options

EUR/USD 5 Minute Chart of Last 12 Hours Price Action

Breakout from consolidation trading range occurs on expansion bar

Breakout confirmed by second five minute expansion bar even larger than first

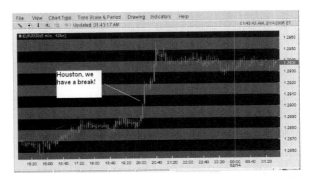

I apologize for the small image size. Don't worry about reading the notes above. Notice the breakout! More importantly, notice the long, tight consolidation pattern beforehand. This is it, baby.

Try to get the bet down before the completion of the second expansion bar, as soon as it becomes obvious that it will satisfy our requirements. Check with the binary options site portfolio page to see the details of your bet and find out what time the current wager is actually settled (which may not be the same time as the ticker shows – this is a big problem in currency betting, by the way, as you can expect the site to determine any "close calls" in their favor, especially if you have been winning lately).

Strategy #1: Mastering the Intraday Breakout

Go lighter on position size than what is recommended for stock index betting, for two reasons:

1.) There are many more trading hours and thus many more playable setups, and thus many more betting situations than with the indices.

2.) You will lose a higher percentage of these bets overall than on the indices. A standard wager size should, therefore, be 8-10% of what your account size was at the beginning of the month as opposed to 12-15% with the indices. You should still be able to show steady profits month in and month out, and by increasing your bet size every month you will get that compounding effect working for you that is so crucial to building wealth. But be aware that breakout plays are more difficult in forex than with indices.

Conclusion

I've seen a lot of advice given on the internet over the years regarding binary options wagering. Much of what is considered to be the better of that counsel often advises to stay away from intraday wagers, describing them as "sucker bets." Even though some of these advisors are obviously smart people, what they are missing is a proper understanding of day trading strategies. Most of them (very likely) don't even have the awareness that profitable day trading strategies exist.

The binary options brokers don't seem to take the threat seriously, either. Even if a few skilled players are beating them on intraday bets, they make so much money from the masses that gamble away their accounts on these wagers that we certainly don't need to worry about them getting turned off. This is a safe strategy for you to master, as in effect you will be paid out of all those gambling losses, which are not likely to dry up anytime soon.

The only drawback is the time factor. You must be available for the high-volume stock market hours every day, and you must be in tune with the current rhythm of the market if you want to bet the indices (which are the most profitable market for this system by a wide margin). A forex player who lives in the U.S. can get up at an ungodly hour in the morning and play when the London market opens; otherwise, he also needs to be available for watching the market during the day. If you can do either (or both) you're in luck, because getting good at this particular "sucker bet" strategy is far and away the coolest way to successful fixed odds binary options wagering.

Strategy #2: High-Odds Big Picture Positioning

Big picture positioning is the number one reason why most people should have a fixed-odds binary options account, regardless of their personal situation. How else can the average Joe position himself to profit from major world economic trends?

I am talking specifically about major price trends in gold, oil, currencies, and the overall stock market. These trends last for years, not weeks. The underlying fundamentals which drive them are rooted deeply in economic conditions that are undeniable. These trends do not significantly reverse without real changes in the political and/or economic climate. When the changes do happen they are gradual, not sudden. The smart financial bettor gets on board not too early, but in plenty of time to cash several consecutive wagers on each major trend.

This strategy has very close to a 100% win rate, but it captures only small percentage gains. Often, they are extremely small. Consequently, this system will not make you wealthy by itself. It is best used as a compliment to your core trading strategies. Understand, though, that when I say small percentage gains, I am still talking about beating the return of the S&P 500 and probably more than tripling the return on your savings account at the corner bank. Otherwise, what would be the point?

Read the Financial News

To work this strategy effectively, you must be up and current with the financial news, particularly world economics. If Asia is in recession you should know it. If the U.S. is experiencing a record increase or decrease in its trade deficit, you need to be aware. Fortunately, all this stuff is available in the business section of any major newspaper, and even more so by watching financial news stations such as Bloomberg and CNBC.

The best trades are created by changing conditions. Old, worn-out trends that were spawned by events and conditions from years gone by are not what we're looking for. It helps to be aware of historical high and low prices as well, as this creates a reference point that can help determine when a new trend has started. As mentioned, however, betting on brand new trends is not recommended. Wait until they become established, noticeable, and are in the news. They can last for years, so you don't need to be early. Jumping the gun can cause you to start predicting things instead of reacting to them. Bet on what is actually happening, not on what you want to see happen.

Tools

Charting. The most useful charts I have seen for currencies, gold, oil, indices, as well as all other types of futures contracts are at barchart.com. Here is a link you can bookmark that will put you right at their futures page:

http://www2.barchart.com/mktcom.asp?code=BSTK&section=currencies

The in-house charts at some of the binary options sites are also quite helpful, as they show you the spot price and draw a line at the price level you are betting on (or for this strategy, against). But some of them only go back about six months, and the Big Picture strategy calls for a longer-term view. You should be plotting your bets on a monthly chart and then be looking for optimal entry points (bounces from corrections) on a weekly chart. Indicators, oscillators, and the like are useless for the long term trades we are making, so leave your chart clean.

Fundamentals. Charts are only one of your tools. In fact, they are only useful as far as choosing the price level to bet against. The reason to pull up a chart in the first place is born on the fundamental picture. When the Yen, Dollar, Gold, Oil, or stock market starts moving strongly, and that move is clearly explainable by political and world economic developments, it's time to perk up and start planning your bet. That's when you break out the chart and look to time your entry.

Betting Logistics

The wager you will be making is the **No-Touch** bet. The best time frame I have found for making these bets is 120 days, which ties up your capital for four months (if you don't sell it back early). Please note you will need to verify that the binary option site you play at offers time frames this long.

What usually happens, if you are doing this right, is the market keeps moving in the obvious direction. If the site you are playing at offers a bet buy-back feature, you are almost always in profit within two months' time. There really isn't much point in selling the bet back early unless the market becomes so overextended that you can get out for most of your originally intended profit. In that case, you can wait for a correction and then get back on board again in the direction of the major trend.

Speaking of corrections, these make the best entry points. Don't expect significant ones, however. Any small countermove in the market is time to get in. By betting on the first such opportunity after you have decided to make the play, you will be squeezing the most out of your return pricing. Use a daily chart if you really want to get surgical with your entry. Don't wait longer than a few days, though, as you want to have a position before the primary trend continues.

The return pricing you get will vary. Expect about 8% on the low side and 20% on the high end. Any less than that just isn't worth it, and any more than 20%

means you are betting too close to the current price and will be in danger of a normal correction causing a loss. You should almost never lose one of these plays. Most of my Big Picture wagers get a 10-12% return for a 120 day term.

The No-Touch price, however, should not be chosen simply by the return. It should be located on the monthly chart at a technical point, usually just beyond what looks to be a major support or resistance level. Once in a while, you will get a 20% return while conforming to these betting logistics. But you will also see 5% prices sometimes, in which case you might just want to forget it for now and wait for the next pullback to try again.

The Setup

Okay, so you heard on the news over the last few weeks that the Dollar, Yen, Gold, Oil, or the stock market has been moving strongly in reaction to some sort of meaningful world event. You've done a little reading on the subject. Whatever this condition is that has developed is pretty serious, and will not be changing any time soon.

You then checked out the monthly and weekly charts for the appropriate futures contract and have confirmed that this looks like the beginning of a major trend, which potentially could move for a long ways based on the past historical highs, lows, and trends of this particular entity.

By the way, if it is the U.S. stock market you are considering a play on, be aware that this is by far the most difficult to assess. The fundamentals behind the move need to be strong, and downtrends are more reliable than up trends. The news or condition driving the move needs to be extremely evident and undeniable. Use the S&P 500 futures contract for charting. Examples of the best playable past trends are when the bubble burst in the tech market in 2000, in which case the NASDAQ was the obvious play, and the post 9-11 environment, in which case the S&P 500 would have been the preferred vehicle.

So now you locate a price level that seems extremely unlikely to be hit anytime soon, given the current conditions, which is beyond a significant support or resistance level on the monthly and/or weekly chart. Price it out for a 120 day wager. Hmmm, 11% return, not bad. But the market has been trading in the direction of the new trend the last couple of days, so wait a couple days to see if a small correction starts and try to eke out a 12-15% return.

What the Past Tells Us

Let's look at some examples now of long-term charts and see where past entries would have made sense. The arrows point to obvious entries, with the horizontal lines at the base of the arrows showing where the approximate No-Touch price levels could have been. Because these are monthly charts, you only have to count four bars to see where the bet would have paid off.

Strategy #2: High-Odds Big Picture Positioning

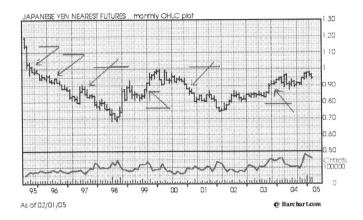

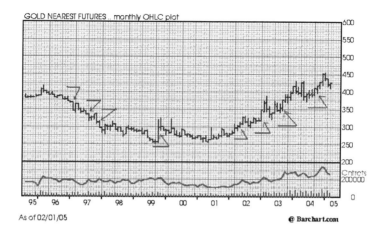

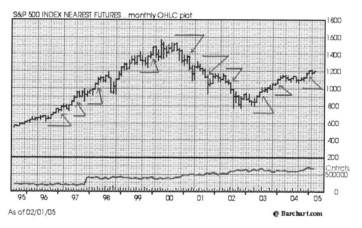

If you'll forgive the crude arrow drawings, you will notice that none of these bets were ever in any real danger of losing. This is because the No-Touch price levels were always far away, beyond technical support or resistance, and in the opposite direction of the major trend. I'm telling you, this is the easiest money

Strategy #2: High-Odds Big Picture Positioning

you will ever make. But you won't make a lot of it, and you will have to wait to be paid.

A few of the bet levels were admittedly drawn so far away from the current price that they may not have been playable, because you just wouldn't have gotten any kind of return. But I'm sure you get the idea. Areas of sideways-trading consolidation make good barriers and you can get closer to the current price when you have one between you, especially earlier in a trend that has strong fundamentals driving it. A weekly chart will allow you to screw down to a better view of where the best level is for pricing the bet.

Don't get greedy and start moving your bet price into the consolidation area in an effort to make more return. It's much more important to have a 100% winning percentage on these plays than to make more return per wager. Hopefully, you now understand that a 100% rate is not only possible, but necessary – as one loss would wipe out many months of profits and turn all your efforts into an exercise in futility. (This is what the binary options broker is counting on. Follow the guidelines just given and you will disappoint them.)

Managing the Position

I will sell a bet back early only if the major trend appears to be topping out from both a fundamental and technical viewpoint, and only if I am getting more than half of my original intended return. This doesn't happen very often, but once in a great while it will.

The news needs to start giving you reason to suspect the trend is over, and a sideways pattern must be forming on the chart that looks as if it is flirting with an opposing-side break.

If all of those conditions are not met, you're better off riding the bet out, as you should be so far away from the No Touch level that you are safe even when a trend reversal starts.

Perhaps the only exception to this is if you are proven dead wrong immediately after establishing the position and the underlying makes an astonishing bee-line straight towards you. In that case, something fundamentally has certainly changed. Find out what it is, reassess the situation, and get out if you can still recoup about half of your wager.

Position Sizing

This trading strategy calls for betting a larger portion of our account balance than any other. The reasons are obvious: A high reliability of winning and a low return rate. It's nice to have a chunk of our account working for us in this manner, even while we are doing other things.

Your optimal bet size is determined by how much of your capital you need available for working other strategies. You also need to have enough on hand for playing any other Big Picture wagering opportunities that appear. If this is the only strategy you want to work, then I would say put 33% of your account balance into each wager, and don't be afraid to have

Strategy #2: High-Odds Big Picture Positioning

three going at once should they be called for. Expect to make about 10-15% annually on your account this way.

You can do much better by working one or two other strategies in this manual as well. In that case, the position size for your Big Picture Positioning wagers should be 15-20% of your account balance, depending on how many other systems you are working and how aggressively you are positioning yourself in those. Always leave room for a string of losses in any of the other strategies without crippling your account too badly.

For simplicity purposes, and for achieving a monthly compounding effect, choose your bet size for this strategy at the beginning of each month and make the same size wager for each and every play which materializes that month.

Conclusion

Don't go overboard with this. Play it the way it is supposed to be played. Insist on fundamentals and wait until a new, strong-acting, long-term trend is confirmed. Put solid support/resistance between your No-Touch price and the market price. Make the market do something simply unbelievable for you to lose. Settle for a small but decent return. Wait the bet out. See what is happening with your eyes and ears, not your imagination. Do these things and you should never lose a bet.

The closest thing to a No-Touch bet in the more traditional financial world would be selling naked option contracts. The primary difference being that those have unlimited risk, whereas these bets have a definable risk.

It's surprising that the binary options sites still give us a decent return (most of the time) on these plays. As already mentioned, they used to give good pricing on short-term No-Touch bets as well, but one day out of the clear blue they just up and turned them off. So there is no guarantee that the Big Picture Positioning plays will stay available indefinitely, either. The binary options brokers do seem likely to let them continue, given the long time commitment of the wagers. Those of us that settle for a reasonable return and put both fundamental and technical factors in our corner will continue to win as long as they still offer them.

Strategy #3: One-Touch Reversal

In the book *How Markets Really Work* by Larry Connors and Conor Sen, fifteen years of recent stock market movements are dissected for the specific purpose of analyzing short-term trends. Short-term meaning time frames from a few days to a couple of weeks. The overwhelming and inescapable conclusion drawn from these statistics is that the overall stock market is much more likely to reverse rather than continue in the same direction after a short-term directional move.

Those findings work out nicely for serious binary options players, because the pricing for One-Touch bets is usually slightly skewed against wagers on the continuation of the latest short-term move. In other words, the return pricing for a One-Touch bet in the opposite direction of the recent trend is normally a little better than the pricing for a bet the same distance in its current direction.

This phenomenon is evident in the options market as well. A stock that is selling for $40 will have a noticeably higher premium for calls at $42.50 than for puts at $37.50 if the price has just run up quickly.

This would be just plain wrong if market movements were actually random. Obviously, the options market prices in a premium for the trending element, be it a fallacy or not.

But wait a minute – isn't the random walk theory a legitimate argument supported by highly intelligent people? Yes, it is. And even though we disagree with their ultimate conclusions, it still benefits us to keep a healthy respect for them at all times. This is one case where we are going to cash-in on that respect. Binary options brokers have a habit of overcompensating in their pricing adjustments when a short-term trend occurs, and we're going to capitalize on it whenever we can.

But the pricing bonus is, simply, a bonus with this strategy. We would be making these bets even if the pricing were about even (and sometimes it is) as long as it is attractive enough for our purposes. A contrarian's approach to recent price movement has its own built-in edge, as demonstrated by the authors of the above mentioned book.

Actually, the binary option brokers may welcome the plays this strategy generates, even if they (correctly) suspect we are getting the best of it. Most market gamblers are trend followers. Part of the reason the pricing may be skewed against the current trend could very well be to attract action on the other side, just as sports books adjust the point spreads in order to "balance the books" as heavily-lopsided action comes in. While pricing models for binaries start in

Strategy #3: One-Touch Reversal

the options market, who knows what the brokers do to it when the books become unbalanced.

Because the individual stocks available for betting usually move more or less in step with the entire market, it does little good to play them individually. This strategy also does not work well on commodities such as gold and oil, as their short-term moves can be unpredictable and will defy all rationalization more often than not. That leaves us with two tradable markets for betting on short-term reversals: indices and currencies.

Getting the Edge

The signals this system generates are based on a technical condition; a definable price action on the chart. Your edge comes from two factors:

1) Statistical evidence that short-term price movements are more likely to reverse than continue

and

2) Your insistence on getting pricing for each wager that forces the winners to ultimately add up to more than the losers cost.

This particular strategy, as presented, only needs to win 40% of the time to be worthwhile. It's important to understand that you can lose more than half of your bets and still be working a winning system. A certain mental realization process is necessary for most people before accepting this concept. Human nature tends to make us think that having less than a 50% win rate is bad. In this case, it's not.

In fact, there are some professionals who trade what is known as a "black swan" system. This is a methodology which takes many, many small losses and then makes it all back plus some on one gigantic win (typically this is a long options strategy). The point is this: all that matters is the bottom line. Our reversal strategy is no black swan system. You will certainly see enough winners to keep you interested, and a steadily increasing account balance to boot.

By now you may be a little confused. If markets are more likely to reverse than continue after a directional move, why does this strategy have less than a 50% win rate? The answer has to do with the pricing we are seeking on our wagers.

Our One-Touch targets are primarily based on technical points on the chart, with bet pricing returns being a secondary condition. Yes, we insist upon a certain return or we won't play – but the payoff level itself is technical. This is absolutely necessary. If we start letting the binary option sites determine our entry and exit points, we will have no chance at beating this game. The knowledge that one outcome is more probable than another is not enough to derive profits from the situation. A strategy or system of some sort must be engineered seeking the optimal performance from maximizing the edge.

Strategy #3: One-Touch Reversal

That's not to suggest this strategy as given can't be improved upon over time in changing market conditions. You probably will be able to do that if you are a serious student of the game. It's just that right now, in the current market climate, I have not been able to adjust it to any better performance level than what is presented below.

Tools

Charting. Any decent chart service, including most of the free ones available on the internet, will do. If you insist, you can use a bar chart – but candlesticks really do tell you more about recent and current market psychology with a quick glance (once you become familiar with them).

Time Frames. Use a daily chart for this strategy. The signals are clearest on a 3-month chart.

Indicators. This system is based on signals that are generated from Bollinger Bands. Specifically, 20-period Bollinger Bands set to 2 standard deviations. Don't worry about these specifications because most sites have them set as their default. But if you are using a charting service that allows you to set the specs, those are the ones you want. Make sure there is a 20-day simple moving average in the middle of the bands.

Betting Logistics

When a signal is issued and a bet is made, most of the time the price of the index or currency will move towards your bet price and actually allow you to sell early for a profit (at the sites which offer this feature). However, most of your bets will not be winners. This is because the price will reverse and move away again before hitting your One-Touch price level about half the time it starts towards it.

But selling your bets early does not make for a winning system, because the amount you win will not pay for the losers. You simply must live and die with the results in order to come out ahead doing this. Your winners will be paying 175% or more profit. That is the minimum. If you can't get at least 175% pricing at the required level, there is no play.

The Setup

The betting signal is as follows:

1. A directional price move on the daily chart touches the upper, lower, or middle band (the middle band is the 20-day moving average).

2. The next day, the price does not trade directionally – that is, it trades sideways and stays about even with yesterday's price range. It is also not completely outside one of the outer bands. Late in the day, when it becomes obvious the price is not expanding nor reversing, but staying about even as yesterday (when the price first touched the band) look to make a bet.

3. Price out the wager in the opposite direction of the recent move. The target is back to the outer or middle band – make sure you have at least six complete trading days to hit it, and are getting at least a 175% return on your wager (for example, risking $50 to win $88). To further clarify: If the signal is at either the top or bottom band, then the target is the middle band. If the signal occurs at the middle band then the target is back towards either the top or bottom band, whichever direction the recent price move came from.

The stall on the day after touching a band is the most important factor. If the price continues in the direction of the recent move, or retreats back in the direction from whence it came, there is no play.

When the price touches one of the outer bands, it has a higher chance of reversing if the band is **mostly horizontal**. When this happens, it is said to collide with the band and it makes a formidable resistance point. By contrast, an outer band that is opening up and going directional with the price is much more likely to see a continued directional price move. By waiting a day and seeing sideways trading, a diagonal band should straighten out some and make the bet look better technically. In any case, only bet on the day that you get sideways trading after the touch.

Any time the price on the next day is outside the outer band and looking like a continued move, stay away! When markets start moving directionally they will go outside the outer bands and ride them, remaining mostly outside the bands, until the next consolidation or reversal period occurs. In an uptrend this is called climbing the ladder, and in a downtrend this is known as sliding down the slippery slope. You want sideways trading the day after the touch – at the band is okay, but not outside of it.

Get six complete trading days to give yourself enough time for the reversal to hit your target. This usually means making an 8-day wager. Beware of upcoming holidays when there is no trading! In that case, you need to expand to a 9-day wager.

Pricing the bets is going to be somewhat ambiguous. You will be looking at where the target band is located currently, but most of the time it will be sloping in one direction or the other – meaning either towards you or away from you. In seeking the 175%+ return you are best off using the level where it is located currently, regardless of its angle. However, sometimes the band will be very close and you will have to make a reasonable extension of the slope to get your pricing. Only do this for one or two days' worth of expected angle extension, only when the target band is unusually close to you, and never increase the current angle. Sometimes in this situation, you will just need to pass on the wager.

Strategy #3: One-Touch Reversal

Here are some examples on a 3-month chart of SPY, mapping the S&P 500.

1. Winner - obvious play, collides with outer band and stalls
2. Winner - trades sideways at, not outside, outer band after touching
3. Winner - hits MA then trades sideways
4. Loser - still was a soild trade once it came back inside outer band
5. Winner - may have been a difficult entry on the long reversal bar
6. Loser - never really penetrated the outer band, but still was a signal
7. Winner - barely touches outer band again, very close and may have lost

The Bollinger bands on the S&P 500 chart above include a continuous moving average, and therefore show good entries for the entire three months.

The EUR/USD currency chart on the next page did not, so the entries are a little hazy at the beginning of the chart.

Beat Binary Options

EUR/USD 3-Month Daily with 20-day Bollinger Bands & 20-day Simple MA

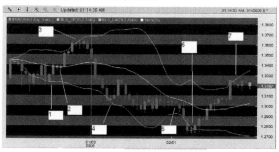

1. Not sure this was really a play, several bars earlier was probably the real play, but either would have won
2. Loser - but perfect setup
3. Winner, classic notice how price did not stall at middle band on the ensuing reversal
4. Loser - probably, but it looked good
5. Winner - although a move up probably was just as likely after the long basing pattern
6. Not really a signal, but after sideways trading back inside the band a savvy player may have bet - and won
7. Inconclusive, one more trading day left, but will probably be a loser

Sorry that the notes in the above image are so small. The important thing is to see the trade entries where the lines are pointing. There are seven plays on this example chart; four of which would have been clear and easy winners.

Both these examples just happen to show more winners than losers, but some of the results would have been close depending on where your exact target price ended up being at. Remember, you only need to win 40% of your bets to be profitable. If you are cashing 40% to 50% of your wagers doing this, which is entirely possible to sustain, then you have a very powerful trading system here.

Many of your losers will trade directionally in powerful trends for a while before they settle down again. You can add something to this strategy by making a reversal bet once you get a couple of days of sideways trading after a strong directional move. Make sure the outside Bollinger Band is starting to flatten out and price comes back inside of it a little, or is at least even with it. This is usually at least as good as the normal signal, as strong price moves normally do see corrections along the way.

This trading strategy is soundly based on statistics – both the statistical evidence that supports price reversal, and the statistics that create the Bollinger Band indicator. By combining both into one trading system, you are giving yourself a statistical edge.

Position Sizing

Most months you will locate 2-3 plays for each market you follow. Ideally, you should follow one stock index and one major currency pair, such as the ones example charts were given for above. This should make for 4-6 wagers total every month, with no more than two bets on at any given time.

That would seem to dictate a large position size. However, a less than 50% win rate means there could be extended stretches of losers from time to time, which advocates backing off on the bet size some. I have found that 10% of account size makes the perfect position size for this strategy. You will be able to survive the occasional bad stretch and still get your money working for you in an optimal way by adhering to this advice. Look to earn a return on your account of about 8% monthly with this system – or about a 120% annual return on your capital when compounded.

For simplicity purposes, and for achieving a monthly compounding effect, choose your bet size at the beginning of each month and make the same size wager for each and every play which materializes that month.

Conclusion

The results this betting strategy will generate for your account are simply outstanding. This system alone is worth many times the price of this manual. You know who makes more than 100% annually on their trading capital? The very top individual traders in existence, that's who. Nobody else! Most professional traders spend their careers trying to come up with a methodology that will generate those kinds of returns, and never do.

The reason hedge fund managers and successful individual traders cannot achieve these kinds of returns is because of the amount of money they have to trade. The more you have, the tougher it is to make high returns. Small accounts can, however, generate these numbers – and in this chapter, I have given you a method for doing just that. When your trading capital reaches a certain level, unfortunately, you will find yourself in the same boat as everyone else. (Unless, of course, you are content to continue trading all of your capital at Binary.com. But this is not wise, as already mentioned, and if you keep beating them at these bets with a $40,000+ account size you can expect them to notice and perhaps kill the golden goose.)

The basics of this system are nothing new. Almost any decent trading book that describes how to use Bollinger Bands – or other types of price channels – will give you the gist of what has been described here. But here's the thing: When you are trading stocks, indices, or currencies in a broker account with this setup, you are not going to make a 175% return on risk capital from your winning trades! Only at a binary options broker is this possible. Of course, in a broker account your losing trades will not always cost you 100% of risk capital, either. Overall, a winning system using this technique in a brokerage account (in the hands of a skilled and disciplined trader) can maybe make a 2-3% gain on capital every month as opposed to the 8% return that binary options players can realize. The leverage is simply better over here.

This strategy is a great springboard system – one that can take the smallest account and grow it exponentially over time. To be successful, you are going to have to get good at it. I have given some very clear-cut, black and white rules regarding trading signals and bet pricing. But you will still find room for discretion when working the system. For example, sometimes the bet target as described will offer 215% return pricing, or even more. Should you shorten the target to say, a 200% or 190% return? Or just roll with the better pricing and figure it will pay off in the long run?

There are no easy answers to questions like this. You need to play with the pricing and get a feel for how the market has been behaving, all the while keeping in mind the overall short-term reversal nature of financial markets. Getting good with the details and learning to work this system effectively will go a very long ways towards your development as a trader, and ultimately your financial security in this life.

Strategy #4: The Index Straddle & Range

The previous chapter described a betting strategy based on a contrarian's approach to recent price movement. This chapter will present a betting strategy that is based on a contrarian's approach to recent volatility. It is a similar strategy statistically speaking, but to the average trader it will probably seem like a completely different concept.

The basic premise behind any contrarian's idea is that whatever has been happening recently is due to stop (at least temporarily), and correspondingly whatever hasn't happened recently is now overdue to happen. Think of the old adage "beware of calm waters" when working this system.

Changing conditions are the defining characteristic of modern financial markets. Ironically, most amateur traders (the ones that have a 90%+ casualty rate) trade in the direction of recent conditions, not against them. Something about "the trend is your friend" and all that. Because this is what most of them do, they pay a heavy premium for their positions. It's a wise trader who fades the crowd and gets good value while doing it.

Let's face it: human nature prods us to bet on the continuation of current conditions. It just seems safer and more comfortable to guess that an index which has been trending will continue to do so, or one that has been constrained to within a 100-point range will remain there. Betting the opposite way puts you out on a ledge all by yourself. When you're wrong and the crowd is right, you might tend to feel silly. I'm here to tell you to get over it. You'll never make any real money betting on what the crowd is betting on.

Similarly, if a particular trading tactic has a 97% success rate and makes a few points every time, but wipes out most of your account balance the rare times it misses, this is a losing system. For every x-number of trials on average you will have a loss on total trading capital. Yet, this is exactly the type of trading many intermediate-level traders pursue, because it registers lots of wins. It feels good. The traders using this type of approach will turn a blind eye to the ever-towering risk that is always standing right behind them, because they can just "feel" they have a winning system. Their focus tends to be on the series of upward movements in their account balance and not the inevitable wipe-out that is always just around the corner. If you take just one thing away from this manual, take this: Do not ever trade this kind of comfortable, losing system – even if the risk and success rate are not as extreme as in this example.

Now consider a trader who is prone to taking the opposite side of those 97% winning trades that were described in the last paragraph. For every x-number

Strategy #4: The Index Straddle & Range

of trials on average he is up on his risk capital. He sees mostly losses, but his account equity ultimately grows. He is a winner. He has found a goose that lays golden eggs. Because he is in the minority camp he gets good value on his positions, sees good fills, has quick executions, and enjoys constant liquidity in his chosen market. Does he have nerves of steel? I don't know, maybe. Perhaps that helps. But even without nerves of steel, someone with a clear understanding of what they are doing and why it works can operate a strategy like this and sleep comfortably at night.

Please understand that I am not saying trend following is useless, or that you should bet against every strong market trend you come across. To the contrary, the Big Picture Positioning strategy in this manual is definitely a trend-following system. But it is a very long-term position strategy, and long-term trends backed by strong fundamentals are quite reliable. Call up a shorter-term chart within any trend and you will see plenty of corrections along the way, some of them severe. This is why trend-trading in the shorter term is so difficult. Getting shaken out of your position on a correction that triggers your stop is the rule, not the exception. And trading without a stop is pure suicide, sooner or later.

As binary options players, we are mostly considering market action over a short term. Therefore, we usually measure price movement and market volatility over the course of hours, days, and maybe weeks on the outside. Because we know the markets zigzag a lot in the short term, and bet pricing is better in the direction opposite the most recent move, it makes sense to formulate a plan that bets on the zig while the market is zagging, and vice-versa.

It is well known that the price movements of financial markets alternate between trending action (directional moves) and range-bound trading. The strategy presented below will have you either betting on a directional move when a market is range-bound, or betting on range-bound market when price is moving directionally. Which one depends on which type of wager is currently being offered at attractive odds.

The Ins and Outs of Straddles

A straddle normally refers to an options spread position where a call and a put are simultaneously purchased at the same strike price. The underlying has to move a certain distance in either direction for the position to show a profit. Otherwise, time decay and low volatility erode the value of the position until both sides eventually expire almost worthless. Normally, if the underlying does make the desired move, the option that is profitable will be liquidated, bringing a profit to the entire position. The other option will be next to worthless and is usually left alone to expire and save the commission. This allows for the occasional instance where the market reverses dramatically – in which case both sides of the spread can be closed at a profit (this is a rare event that produces stellar returns when it happens).

Strategy #4: The Index Straddle & Range

A short straddle is the opposite position as described above – both options are sold instead of bought. In this case, the seller is betting that the price will remain close to the strike price, with time and lack of volatility working in his favor. Once the price moves past a certain distance, a short straddle position will start losing money. A short strangle position is a little more workable. This allows both sides of the spread to expire worthless and so the entire premium collected from the sale can be kept as profit. Instead of using the same strike price, two different strike prices are chosen, both out of the money, with the current security price located between them.

At the binary options sites we can play straddles the same way, but of course instead of buying options we are placing One-Touch bets. One is made above the current price betting on an upward movement, and at the same time another bet is made the same distance below the current price betting on a downward movement. The bets are priced in such a way that if either one wins, a profit from the entire position will be realized. Once in a great while, a wild, gyrating market will hit both touches and we will win both bets, causing us to do the happy dance.

Our version of a short strangle position is the Range wager that most fixed-odds binary option sites offer. Two price levels are selected for this wager, one above and one below the current security price. If either of these levels is breached during the wager period, the bet loses. Time and low price volatility will put this position into profit.

Tools

Charting. Any decent chart service, including most of the free ones available on the internet, will do. If you insist you can use a bar chart, but candlesticks really do tell you more about recent and current market psychology with a quick glance (once you become familiar with them).

Time Frames. Use a daily chart for this strategy. The signals are clearest on a 3-month chart.

Indicators. The only indicator I put on my charts for this strategy is a 20-day moving average. It doesn't matter whether it is a simple moving average or an exponential moving average. It isn't necessary to even use this indicator. On the other hand, if you like throwing other stuff on the chart that shouldn't hurt, either. These wagers are made based on recent price action alone.

Economic Calendar. You will need an economic calendar to work the straddle setup. These can be found at many free financial websites, such as the Yahoo! Finance site.

Betting Logistics

While this strategy can be played on any of the binary option markets, it is particularly effective on the NASDAQ and DAX indices. Those are the only markets I play it on. The NASDAQ is the most volatile of the stock indices, and it also sees the most changes in short-term volatility, which is what we are betting

Strategy #4: The Index Straddle & Range

on. You may very well be able to adjust this system for profitable use on one of the currency pairs; the USD/YEN appears to be the best candidate.

It has been my experience that the binary option brokers will not offer the pricing necessary for both of these setups at any given time. You will either be in a straddle-betting mode or a Range-betting mode, depending on current conditions. You will only being making one type of play or the other until the binaries brokers change the pricing payouts again, in which case you will (hopefully be able to) revert back to the other wager type. These phases last for months at a time, and sometimes one will be "turned off" before the other gets turned on, forcing gaps in your playing time with this system. That can't be helped. Understanding this and acting accordingly is critical to your success.

I once subscribed to a betting signal service that had an impressive track record. We were making almost all Range plays on the indices and were producing steady monthly profits. The way their bets were set up, we were consistently getting around a 75% return on bet pricing and were winning at a 60% rate. After a few happy months of this, the pricing started dropping on the Range wagers for the price levels we were used to playing at. The service continued to issue signals even though we were now only getting about 55% return pricing. The win rate remained at 60%, so we were then all trading a losing system. The service had no plans, nor presented any ideas, on how to combat the changing conditions that were affecting the Range-wager pricing. I discontinued my subscription, as I'm sure many of their other clients did (the smart ones, anyway).

What I'm giving you here is a way to deal with the problem we encountered above. By having two opposing setups, we can ride out the times the binary brokers decide to shake out the winning players, like they apparently decided to do to that particular signal service. (It also really helps to have so many different binary brokers to choose from these days.) I have seen short periods when neither of the following setups was available, but those times have always been brief and usually result in the other becoming available within a few weeks' time. At the time of this writing the Range plays are on, so we'll start with those.

Setup #1 – Index Range

The betting signal is as follows:

1. Expansion bar or candle that is the largest of the last 7 days appears...

2. ...or three days in a row (or more) of directional, higher-high or lower-low closes occurs.

3. The following day (after either of the above two signals appears) sees a calm, sideways trading day that stays about even with the previous close.

4. Price out a Range bet getting 100% return or more that would constrain the price movement to within a range that at least half of the like movements which you see on the three month chart would stay within. Take the shortest time frame available for getting your pricing, which is probably about seven complete trading days after the day you place the bet (often displayed as nine days on the betting menus, depending on upcoming holidays and what day of the week it is).

To make sure the betting day's price action does not expand further or significantly reverse direction, you should make the bet late in the trading session if you are able. Understand that it's the calm, sideways day after a sudden move that sets us up for a minor reversal, which we hope will result in range-bound trading in the immediate future.

The edge this setup provides should be obvious. If the range you are choosing would constrain at least half of all the 7-day price action combinations you see on the current chart, and you are getting 100% pricing or better, viola!

Here are some examples on a chart:

1. Entry at 2120, Lost (barely)
2. Entry at 2160, Won
3. Entry at 2160, Lost
4. Entry at 2090, Won
5. Entry at 2025, Won (barely)
6. Entry at 2085, Won
7. Entry at 2085, Lost
8. Entry at 2030, Won (barely)

At the time of this writing, with the NASDAQ in the 4200 area, these plays are setting up well with the barriers 75 points in either direction (for a 150-point total range). Most wagers are eking out a smidgeon over 100% pricing, and they are winning at a 55-60% rate. How long these conditions will last is yet to be seen. Should they prove to be short-lived, I stand waiting in the wings to apply the next setup, which almost always opens up when this one closes.

Setup #2 – Index Straddle

The betting signal is as follows:

1. Several days of calm, sideways trading – the longer the better.

2. Tomorrow is an important economic number reporting day...

3. ...**or** any other potential market-moving catalyst happens tomorrow.

4. Price out two One-Touch bets at an equal distance from the current market price, one above and one below. Get 300% return pricing on each bet at price levels that are foreseeably obtainable. In other words, the move needed to win will not be larger than all such moves you see on the chart currently (there must be at least one move within the last three months that was larger than what you are now betting on). Make sure you have at least six complete trading days to hit your bet.

You should make the bet late in the trading day, if you are able, to confirm that today's price action was constrained. The longer price has been in a somewhat-tight range, the more likely it is to move.

The type of economic numbers that are most likely to move the market depend on the current environment somewhat, so you need to be up on the financial news. But the biggies are usually the Unemployment Rate,

PPI (Producer Price Index), CPI (Consumer Price Index), and FOMC Policy Decisions (the Fed deciding what to do with short term interest rates).

Political events such as war news and elections are also terrific catalysts. Pay attention to the news, watch for upcoming events, and you will find others. Just don't forget that you need a quiet trading period before making a wager. Quiet trading acts as a springboard for the next move. Here are some examples on a chart:

1. PPI - this would have won
2. CPI - this should have won, close & hard to tell for sure
3. Quiet Holiday trading before the New Year deserves a play, wow!
4. PPI - should have won, notice nice long consolidation period
5. FOMC policy decision, this probably would have lost
6. Unemployment Rate, winner
7. PPI again, winner again, market has inflation jitters
8. Unemployment rate, no effect will likely lose but time left

At the time of this writing, the binary options sites are not quite offering the pricing we need for straddles. With the NASDAQ hanging around the 4200 level, 6-

trading day One-Touch bets are now returning about 260% for a 120-point move and we need to get 300% for that. This is a somewhat subjective decision, and you will need some experience working this strategy before it becomes second-nature to you. But look at the move after example #7 above. On this chart, that's the size move that seems reasonable, and it was only about 70 points total (both sides, as we were going 35 points in each direction back when the example index was trading around 2100). The move you are asking for needs to be attainable without being a newsworthy event.

The reason you must insist upon 300% pricing for each bet is because this makes it an even-money proposition. For example, risking $100 on each bet will cost $200 on the losers, but a winner will return a $200 total profit (disregarding the rare double-touch winner). Your goal is simply more than a 50% win rate.

It is entirely possible to adjust the One-Touch levels and accept different pricing to try and hit a different winning percentage. I must warn you, though, that I have done this and have not found anything better than simply going with the 300% pricing and more than 50% winners goal. Taking 200% pricing means you need to win more than 2/3 of the time, and I have found that this system underperforms. My belief is that it's because there are not enough market moves that fall short and reverse to make up for the lower return. However, there is good evidence that you could design a method of getting something like

1200% pricing (on the high-yield wagers, if you can find them) and trying for a win rate of around 13%. But most people will give up on such a methodology before it bears fruit. All things considered, I recommend going with the 300%/50% strategy just described.

Position Sizing

With an average number of monthly bets around two and a 50%+ win rate, this strategy calls for a large position size. Bet 15% of your account balance on each play. That's each play, not each wager. So make the Range bets 15% of your account, but the straddles should be around 7.5% of your account on each side.

The exception, of course, if is you are also working other strategies that are tying up your capital. Especially if you are making 1-Touch Trend Reversal plays from the previous chapter at the same time. In that case, you should ease off a little on the bet size to reduce market risk at any given time.

For simplicity purposes, and for achieving a monthly compounding effect, choose your bet size at the beginning of each month and make the same size wager for each and every play which materializes that month.

Conclusion

Strategy #4: The Index Straddle & Range

Why are both setups never seemingly available for playing at the same time? I don't know exactly, but I have plenty of suspicions. Perhaps the binary options pricing platform (that is now shared by multiple binary brokers) is adjusting the pricing intentionally. Just when one group gets good at one type of strategy they screw down the pricing on them. By then, hopefully the players are addicted to the bet type and will continue to play what is now a losing game, as the signal service I told you about at the beginning of this chapter did. In the meantime, they need to get a new group of players hooked on something. They can't turn the pricing back up on the group they are now milking to death yet, so they turn it up on the opposing types of bets and start the cycle again with a new bunch of players. Get them hooked, and then fix the game on them. This is a bit analogous to how a heroin dealer operates, unfortunately, but it is one possibility. Then again, maybe I'm being paranoid.

It could all be due to market dynamics. Market conditions are always changing. The binary options pricing engines are based on options pricing models. Options traders will tell you about strategies that used to work, just like the stories long-time binaries players will tell. Successful option traders are forced to roll with the changes and continually adapt new strategies if they want to survive. Buy when prices are cheap, sell when prices are expensive, all the while strictly controlling risk and insisting on having a perceived edge.

Perhaps it is a combination of these two concepts?

In any case, you will only play the strategy that is currently "on" as defined by the available wager pricing. Sometimes neither strategy will be available to play. When that happens, give these systems a rest and check back in a couple of weeks.

This strategy will only produce a couple of bets per month on average, regardless of what mode we are currently in. If you are betting 15% of your account balance and winning 60% of your wagers on an even money proposition, that is about a 3% monthly return, or 40% annually after compounding. (These figures do account for the times that neither setup is available and also for the times that the straddles will double-touch win.)

Before you dismiss such potential results as not being worth your while, reflect a moment upon all the failed traders and binary option players chasing extremely high returns. Or I should say, were chasing high returns, before they blew their accounts out. A 40% annual compounding return will make you wealthy in 10-15 years, even if you are starting with next to nothing now. Most money managers would give their back teeth for such a performance. You, a skilled, small-time individual trader, can do it. I have just shown you how.

Keep in mind that some binary options brokers will permanently turn off any wagering opportunities that a small group of players learn how to exploit for large returns. There is no need to dream of such unattainable things. The best – and only sustainable

Strategy #4: The Index Straddle & Range

— approach is to siphon off a small steady stream of monthly profits, ultimately paid for by all the gamblers out there. The binary options brokers may even welcome your contrarian action as you help reduce their overall market risk exposure. Do that, and a few years from now you will be sitting on a large pile of cash — and everyone (including your binaries broker) will be wondering how you did it.

Strategy #5: Price Tracking for Value

For some reason or another, bet price anomalies do appear rather frequently in the binary options pricing engines. They occur often enough for a worthwhile return to be made by a savvy player who is paying attention. Maybe it's an occasional pricing-system glitch that causes it. Or perhaps it is an intentional effort to attract wagers on the other side of positions they have a large exposure on. Whatever the reason, it creates an opportunity for us, one which this chapter will show you how to cash in on.

To work this strategy, you will have to abandon the idea of predicting market direction. You must not care about looking into your crystal ball and then being proven correct. (That's usually an exercise in futility, anyway.)

When your price tracking unveils a value bet, be prepared to jump on it – regardless of what market you find it in or what direction the bet is in. This is all about getting the best of it, not handicapping the market. The binary options site doesn't know any more than you or anyone else about what direction any particular market is heading. They have no inside information and the value bet they are temporarily offering is not a "trap." Rest assured these offerings **will** be temporary and you need to act fast when you find one.

The reason these off-priced wagers are worth playing is because the binary-pricing platforms usually do an admirably efficient job on pricing. Their bet offers are normally priced just a little below where fair value is, netting themselves a small but formidable edge. When you see something significantly out of whack with what they have been offering recently, or with similar wagers they are currently offering in the other direction, it is normally safe to assume you can gain the edge by taking the offer.

That doesn't mean you are going to win the bet, of course. But you should win enough of them to show a profit on average. It's important to make sure the bet being offered is significantly off the norm, not just slightly off. Nobody is forcing you to make a play, so wait until something juicy is being dangled in front of you. Even if you only come up with two or three per month, it is still well worth doing the legwork to locate them.

These plays will be all over the board in terms of return pricing and time frames. Therefore, it is hard to predict a win rate and average monthly return. Use a good position sizing strategy and play them in any time frame and for any price that looks like a great value. The type of bet you will be using is the One-Touch wager. (Although you can conceivably play

Strategy #5: Price Tracking for Value

pricing anomalies using any of the wager types, with the probable exception of the intraday contracts.)

Before you can know what constitutes a value bet, you will have to be tracking prices for a while. You may need several sheets of data for reference before becoming confident enough to start making wagers. So, plan on at least a month of preparation before you can really start working this system.

Unfortunately, the price data gathering process must be done during market hours. If you do it when the market is closed, you may indeed find good setups – but they will likely be gone by the time you log on after the market reopens. If you don't have time for this during stock market hours, you can always track a couple of major currency pairs when you get home from work.

Tools

Price Chart. This is something you design and make for yourself. Excel spreadsheets work well, or you can just draw some lines for columns and rows on a piece of paper. What you want is to have a place for writing bet return prices at several different increments above and below the current price of each entity you are tracking. Design it in a way that will allow all the markets you follow to be tracked. This will take more than one sheet if you are tracking both indices and major currency pairs.

First determine what increment levels above and below the current price you want to track. For example, if you are tracking indices you may want to track three prices at different increments above and below the current price of each index (this has worked well for me in the past). Because the price levels worth keeping tabs on will be different for each index, you should decide what they are individually and assign a number for each increment. This will be necessary in order to build a simple price tracking chart.

Here are the increments for the major U.S. indices that I recommend at the time of this writing (in the spring of 2014).

Increments	DOW	S&P	NASDAQ
1	150	15	40
2	200	20	55
3	300	30	75

Now you can build a simple price-tracking chart based on the values you have assigned as increments. You want to track these increments both above and below the current entity price. So with three increments as selected above, you have six prices to take note of for each underlying. Log these bet prices in however often you decide to track prices. I find that once per market day will usually uncover the anomalies. However, you may be able to pick up an

Strategy #5: Price Tracking for Value

extra one here and there by doing it twice per day, especially in a very active and directional market. In that case, I would take the first readings early in the day and the second during the last trading hour.

Here is what your price tracking chart for the index tracking setup we are developing will start to look like.

Index	Up 1	Up 2	Up 3	Down 1	Down 2	Down 3
DOW						
S&P						
NASDAQ						

You need to repeat those rows for the Indices over and over until you fill the page, because this small sample ignores the wager time frames. You will need a separate matrix to fill for each bet time frame you want to track (5 days, 14 days, etc.).

Here is a more complete example that includes three matrixes for three different wager time frames:

Wager	Index	Up 1	Up 2	Up 3	Down 1	Down 2	Down 3
6 Day	DOW						
6 Day	S&P						
6 Day	NASDAQ						
14 Day	DOW						
14 Day	S&P						
14 Day	NASDAQ						
30 Day	DOW						
30 Day	S&P						
30 Day	NASDAQ						

In case your brain hasn't put this all together quite yet, the empty spaces are where you write in the bet return pricing for each increment you are tracking.

For example, in the empty space for 6 Day DOW Down 2: My chosen increment for DOW 2 is 200 in the first table, above. Therefore, in this space we write down the current return pricing offered for a 6-day One-Touch wager 200 points lower than where the DOW is currently trading.

The price chart is the only tool used for this strategy. You can, of course, put whatever entity you are tracking on a chart to see what it looks like before placing a bet, just to make sure you do not vehemently disagree with the technical situation. If you are a good technician, this may improve your performance. (In my experience, adding technical analysis to this system works best with currencies and especially individual stocks.)

The Setup

The trading signal is when you suddenly get offered a bet return price much larger than what it has been lately for one **and only one** of the figures in your chart. You want the wager that is obviously out of whack and likely offering good value at the moment. This means you must ignore the times that all pricing suddenly gets better, as that doesn't mean a thing. It could be the result of changes in volatility, or perhaps the pricing was bad before and the binaries pricing platform is now looking to increase wagering action by offering almost-fair prices.

Let's look at an actual example I found on our index tracking system using a **7-day wager**.

Index	Up 1	Up 2	Up 3	Down 1	Down 2	Down 3
DOW	38%	84%	245%	41%	91%	261%
S&P	31%	69%	192%	39%	82%	218%
NASDAQ	58%	99%	187%	58%	99%	182%
DOW	42%	86%	248%	37%	94%	259%
S&P	34%	67%	195%	39%	83%	214%
NASDAQ	55%	95%	188%	60%	102%	188%
DOW	36%	92%	260%	39%	86%	248%
S&P	42%	73%	198%	33%	77%	210%
NASDAQ	54%	92%	180%	61%	106%	191%
DOW	44%	90%	252%	40%	88%	257%
S&P	40%	79%	210%	35%	71%	199%
NASDAQ	58%	100%	183%	58%	97%	189%
DOW	39%	83%	265%	36%	96%	250%
S&P	34%	84%	217%	40%	68%	194%

Strategy #5: Price Tracking for Value

NASDAQ	62%	104%	192%	55%	94%	184%
DOW	37%	82%	238%	41%	**137%**	269%
S&P	31%	79%	212%	43%	72%	199%
NASDAQ	60%	98%	191%	56%	100%	187%

The increment number for each index is the one to compare. So you are scanning down the columns, not across the rows. Compare all 1's to 1's, both up and down. Compare 2's to 2's and 3's to 3's. In the above example, the signal is bolded and enlarged so it jumps out at you – which it should do anyway, being such a better price than normal. On this chart, the average return for a 2 increment move on the DOW for a 7-day *One-Touch* wager has been running between 80% and 100%. To get a sudden offer of 137% is a clear standout and is screaming to be played.

You will have to decide just how far off the norm an offer needs to be in order to warrant a play. In the example given, the wager is returning 40% more than the high end of the average recent range. That much of a difference simply **must** be giving you an edge. My suggestion is to seriously look at any offers where the return pricing is suddenly 25% higher than the upper recent range.

Position Sizing

You will find clear standouts, as in the above example, fairly consistently. The more data you are willing to track (markets, increments, and time frames) the more good wagers you will find. The more wagers you are finding, the less you should bet on each one.

If you are finding 2-3 good set-ups per month, then bet about 15% of your portfolio on each play. If you are getting 4-6 bets down monthly, reduce that amount to about 10%. Bet at least 8% of your account size per play no matter how many plays you are discovering. Keep in mind that if you are finding a lot of them, then they are no longer anomalies and you should tighten up your criteria so that you are only jumping on the very best, most out-of-synch offers.

For simplicity purposes, and for achieving a monthly compounding effect, choose your bet size at the beginning of each month and make the same size wager for each and every play which materializes that month.

Conclusion

One of the side benefits of working this strategy is that it's great basic training for becoming a successful trader. Choosing a system for locating trade entries is not as important as making sure the methodology behind the system is giving you an edge. Likewise, actual results in the short run are not that important either. Having an edge is what is important.

Strategy #5: Price Tracking for Value

There are many ways to gain an edge trading in the financial markets. Yet most people still fail. That's because there's more to trading than locating entries. Position sizing and position management are actually more critical than trade entries. At binary options sites, you are relieved of the position management task, as once you make a bet you're almost always forced to live or die with the results. (The sites that offer bet buy-backs pretty much only offer them at prices you won't want to sell at.) So learn to hone your craft by developing trade entry criteria and applying optimal position sizes.

This strategy is a pure method of locating edges. It ignores everything else. You can't let an opinion about market direction get in your way, as it will sabotage your results. When you are offered a proposition that gives you an edge, jump on it. Similarly, if a co-worker offers you 12-10 odds on a Superbowl wager (against the actual current point-spread), take it – even if you are betting against your favorite team.

Sometimes you may find value wagers that are opposing existing positions this system generated earlier. That should be a rare occurrence, and there will always be a time differential between the conflicting bets. Go ahead and make those conflicting plays when this happens. Being able to do so, without reservation, will help you develop the proper mindset for playing a winning system.

Learn to care only about getting the best of it, while practicing sound risk control principles, and you will be well on your way to building wealth or income through successful speculation. Working a price-tracking strategy at your favorite binary options site will drill this critical concept home, and make the remainder of your trading education easier (and significantly less expensive) than it would perhaps otherwise be.

Developing Your Binary Options Business Plan

Why Bother? Because most successful financial endeavors are the result of following a written business plan. Many failed ventures are the direct result of not having a well-defined plan. The people who win consistently at probability games, such as poker or trading in the financial markets, are those that treat it as a business. To be successful at this particular type of business, you really need to know what you are doing and why. When you know what you are doing and why, you acquire a calm confidence, and do not become frustrated by the bad spells which must occur – and are, in fact, accounted for in advance by a well thought-out business plan.

 Otherwise, it's just too easy to get distracted from your purpose. There are many ways to abandon your original intentions and start gambling without an edge at the binary options sites. Making frivolous wagers because you are chasing recent losses is the number one reason why otherwise decent players blow out their accounts. But there are other ways of becoming derailed as well – like increasing your bet size due to overconfidence from recent wins, or acting on a hunch you acquired from information you read in the paper or overheard on Bloomberg. Having a written business plan and reviewing it regularly is a good way to keep yourself on track and moving toward your objectives.

Define Your Objectives

The first step in putting your binary options business plan together is to define your objectives. What do you want from your account? Income? Growth? Or is it just another weapon in your trading arsenal? (Hopefully, your objective is exponential account growth, to the point where you can graduate from binary options and then keep a small amount there as that extra weapon.) Whatever it is you seek, you are much more likely to accomplish it if you write it down. By doing so you will have decided that this is what you want, and will have established a clear target.

Be careful not to set your expectations unreasonably high. For example, a steady 30% monthly return playing the Intraday Breakout and Price Tracking strategies is unrealistic and not going to happen. The only way you're going to figure out what kind of income to expect is to get good at your strategies, put lots of carefully-planned wagers on, and then look at the results. For that reason, I recommend not setting a percentage or dollar amount goal, especially in the beginning. Stick with your best wagers and your account **will** grow. Don't worry about how much. A somewhat vague objective such as "a steadily rising account balance while also learning to get in tune with the financial markets" is much better than trying to hit some return on capital figure that you chose out of thin air.

You should include the Big Picture Positioning strategy in your business plan, no matter which other strategies you are into. Don't get so caught up in day to day details that you forget to back up and look at the weekly and monthly charts once in a while, for all the markets. Pay attention to the financial news in search of new developing major trends. These plays are free money and you should always have a small portion of your account tied up in them, as a sort of interest-earning cash reserve.

Creating Your Roadmap

Create a new Word or spreadsheet file and name it something like "Binary Options Business Plan" (or just title a piece of paper that you will keep near your computer). Call the first section "Objective" or "Goal" and write what you have decided your objective is.

Note the date that you are starting the plan and what your current account balance is. Then describe your strategy for accomplishing your objective (which strategies you are going to work and for how long). Anytime you make a deposit or withdrawal note the date, amount, and resulting new account balance.

Occasionally, you may decide to alter your strategy, or maybe scrap it entirely and begin with a new one. In fact, arriving at a point where you can do just that may be part of your original plan. If that's the case, simply make another note and describe the new strategy when the time comes.

It doesn't need to be fancy, just a series of notes that define your current objective and your plan to get there. You also want to be able to get a clear picture of your progress with a quick look. On the next page is an example using a spreadsheet format.

Developing Your Binary Options Business Plan

Binary Options Business Plan

Objective: Earn steady monthly returns while developing a sixth sense for my markets

Date	+/-	Balance	Strategy
1/1/14	+$500	$500	1-Touch Trend Reversals on the S&P500 and Intraday Breakouts on the EUR/USD
3/12/14	+$100	$500	
5/17/14		$732	NASDAQ Straddles / Range bets and Intraday Breakouts on the EUR/USD
7/6/14		$916	
9/20/14	-$100	$1014	
12/1/14		$1273	Price Tracking the Indices and Intraday Breakouts on the EUR/USD

As you can see, this player had an initial drawdown when he began playing (which is quite common, even for good traders), but within a couple of months started earning a steady return on his account. It's easy to see how he's doing it, how he's done lately, and what his current objectives are, all at a glance.

The last entry shows a new strategy aimed at finding value bets in the indices while still concentrating on his specialty of day trading the EUR/USD currency pair. He has tried several strategies on the stock market, and now decided he just wants to stick with value bets there, without the need for charting it. Notice the apparent logical steps that were used in slowly stepping up the bet size as to not put too much stress on the account at any given time.

This is a realistic business plan that is very close to the one I used to initially get my account off the ground. The only criticism I have is that it is completely dependent on the initial account size, and even withdrew the additional deposit made when things started picking up. At this juncture, it's obvious the trader has developed the skills and discipline needed to be profitable. It's time to start making additional monthly deposits to turbo-charge the account growth.

Using Your Roadmap

The purpose of having this business plan is to keep you focused on your objective. You should, therefore, refer to it often so you don't forget what your purpose is and stray off course. I suggest making a ritual of reviewing it before you start searching for trade setups. As you can see, it won't take but a few seconds, and this kind of mental reinforcement will bolster your fortitude.

People do not plan to fail, but many fail to plan. Betting on the financial markets is fun. Treating it like a business and seeing how well you can do by adhering to a wisely conceived plan is even more fun (if you ask me).

Beat Binary Options

Onward and Upward to Real Trading

Don't take the title of this final chapter the wrong way! If you have learned to beat binary options consistently, you've accomplished a great mental feat that is not to be downplayed or compared in a negative light to trading a brokerage account. Quite the contrary – beating binary options is at least as difficult as becoming a profitable trader in the real world. When you have this bucket shop wagering conquered, you will have developed the same set of skills necessary for successful trading with larger sums of money in broker accounts. This has been a fantastic training ground. You do have some graduate work ahead of you, but the odds of success are now strongly on your side.

The most important skills you have learned are discipline and having an emotionally-detached view of the markets. These things are crucial. They are more important than actual trading strategies by miles. Truth be told, profitable trading strategies aren't that hard to come by. I've provided a handful in this manual. But I cannot make you apply them correctly. That part is up to you. Either you have what it takes to stay focused and work a system, or you don't. If you are prone to developing opinions about what the market is going to do, and then sticking with them like glue, then I would have to bet against your success as a trader. Successful traders don't become married to positions, nor do they let their opinions about market direction blind them to what is happening on the chart or with current derivatives pricing. Making a bet in the opposite direction of what I personally feel the market is going to do is a very common play for me.

There is another skill worth mentioning, that of understanding which strategies meld with your personality and market perspective (not just your time constraints). Don't fight this – if it doesn't come naturally, if the strategy doesn't just click into place with a light bulb going off above your head, it probably isn't for you. You should feel some excitement about the strategies you choose to pursue. The top traders all have a passion for the markets that cannot be extinguished by mere losing trades.

By now you should understand that consistent profits are only taken out of the markets by playing a highly-disciplined game. Emotions have no place here, except to make the binary brokers more profitable. You simply cannot double your bet size because this next setup looks much better than the last six or seven, or because you are due for a win. You **must** maintain your pre-elected position size for any strategy you are working, or you are lost to the dark side. Just one breach and you have opened Pandora's

Box. I mean it. Don't do it. Don't start fudging on your entry requirements, either. It's much more important to preserve capital than it is to get money into action. Believe me, as I know from hard experience. Don't listen to the devil on your shoulder.

The secret to winning is, ironically, to stop caring about whether you win the next bet or not. This can be a dangerous statement to those not ready for it, so let me explain. You have pre-defined conditions that say bet. When those conditions appear you bet. There is no real judgment involved, even when you are working a system that requires some subjectivity in calling the entries. You do the best you can and learn as you go. Don't beat yourself up, just get better. Either the conditions fit your current betting criteria or they do not. If you're losing too many bets, or trading an unprofitable system, then it's time to change the conditions which say bet. That's all there is too it. Decisions about what makes a good trade are not to be determined when searching for bet conditions. They need to be defined ahead of time, after market hours. Once you have a winning set of criteria you simply stick with it until it stops working, at which time you define a new set of winning criteria (if available).

If you have made it this far, congratulations! Your account has reached $10,000 or more and you are ready to start trading in the real world. You've obviously gotten in synch with your markets, and you've made discipline your bedfellow. There are some new concepts you are going to have to learn to deal with, the most important being that of position management.

Managing Positions

At the binary options sites you enjoyed the cushy situation of never (or almost never) having to worry about managing positions. You defined the conditions of a bet that had an edge, and when those conditions appeared you bet your standard position size for that month. That was the end of it, and you were always willing to die with the wager. Your position size strategy took care of position management in its entirety.

There is one way of trading in the real world that allows you to ignore position management as well: long options strategies. Specifically, buying out-of-the-money options. Usually way out-of-the-money, costing less than $25 per contract (or less than .25 on the options chain quote). There are profitable strategies that can be developed which do this and only this. It's virtually the same thing as playing binary options from a risk management perspective, as you must be willing to die with the position when you make the trade. Consequently, each trade must be of a conservative size. This is, however, a methodology that loses most plays and makes it back on the few that hit. Most people just can't handle this type of trading, so it's not recommended for everyone.

Why limit yourself to just one club in your trading golf bag, anyway? After all, you are graduating, right?

There's a whole lot more out there in the trading world that you now deserve to have access to. Unfortunately, most of it is dangerous – chiefly because it will now involve managing your open positions.

Understand that most amateur traders fail. The overwhelming reason for that is they do not properly manage their positions. Also realize that no one plans to mismanage their position on any particular trade. It just sort of happens. Market conditions are always changing, and thus it becomes easy to justify letting a losing trade remain open by some criteria not considered when the trade was entered, such as, "It's now nearing a strong support area," or other such nonsense.

Letting a losing position get out of hand will kill you. I say this knowing full well that right now, as you are reading this, you plan to never let a losing position get out of hand. But let me tell you, so did every losing trader who blew their account out. Is your resolve that much stronger than theirs? Not likely. You worked so hard to build your bankroll! I don't want you to lose it in a brokerage account and have to start over again with binaries, which is an all-too-real possibility. So listen, understand, and apply these next two words: **Stop Loss**.

Just knowing those two words is not going to save you. The 90% of traders who blew their accounts out knew them also. But you have something else going for you. You have a discipline that allowed you to build a large binary options account. You have practiced using that discipline to a degree that should, by now, make it second-nature to your trading. So when you set a stop loss, you will abide by it. You will never adjust it after a trade has been opened. If you just follow through with that one commitment, you will never blow up as a trader. You will be safe. Your bankroll will survive no matter what.

Just where to set a stop loss is dependent on your particular trading strategy. But I can give you some very helpful hints. Buy at support, go short at resistance, and set the stops just on the other side of those areas. Make sure you have a reasonably attainable profit target of 2-3 times your stop loss (such as the Bollinger band strategy described in the One-Touch Trend Reversal chapter, where the middle band is the target). Always obey your stops. Always. One slip-up and you will be seriously close to becoming lost to the dark side. And when the dark side claims you, it's just a matter of time before your entire account evaporates.

Stop losses must be obeyed. A sensible method of taking profits must also be employed. Usually, you want to cut losses short and let profits run. This can only be accomplished by using a *trailing stop*. A trailing stop is just what it sounds like. You continue to move the stop towards the security price after you are in profit, but always still allowing some wiggle room. This way you can catch the really big moves but still get out with some profit on the moves that start but then fail. The trailing stop is the primary tool of the trading professional – make it yours as well.

It is critically important to allow winning trades to run for a reasonable distance, as the occasional home run is where most of your profits will ultimately come from. In order to do this, you must be willing to lose back much of your initial gain. Think of it as playing with the house's money. Keep your trailing stop back far enough that random market noise won't hit it when you first move into profit. Don't become frustrated when a trade is a big winner but then reverses and hits your trailing stop for a very minimal gain. You enter trades for technical reasons and you must exit them for technical reasons as well. The chart must be telling you the trade failed, or has reached another support/resistance area and has lost its directional bias, before getting out.

When you graduate to trading a broker account, you will find yourself facing many choices as far as trading vehicles go. Becoming adept at binary wagering will have prepared you particularly well for a certain type of trading: options. This is true regardless of which market you specialize in. While most new options traders fail, you will have an edge because you already have mastered avoiding all the usual pitfalls that victimize the uninitiated. You unknowingly have become a skilled options trader while building your binary options account.

Option Trading vs. Binary Options Betting

As previously mentioned, being a binary options player is similar to being an options buyer. Most options trading literature will condemn option buying as a gamblers' folly that is doomed to eventual bankruptcy. These books and articles will explain how 90% of options expire worthless and how the crowd loses untold millions, all of it going to option sellers. Naturally, they go on to recommend option selling as the only approach that has an edge, and teach spread strategies as a method of controlling risk.

While there is merit in some of the option-selling tactics that are widely recommended in the trading literature, the theory behind it is quite spurious. We are told to sell options because the "crowd," who are a described as a bunch of losers, buy them. I'm here to tell you that there is also a very large crowd selling options these days, maybe even larger than the crowd that buys them. This is no doubt due to so many publications touting option selling as the way to go. Nassim Taleb, professional trader and author of the excellent book *Fooled by Randomness*, says that in his 30 years as a trader almost every single professional options trader he ever met "specialized" in selling options. Taleb specialized in buying them. The overwhelming majority of these option selling traders he met were not around very long, blowing up like a string of firecrackers.

Trading isn't easy, as you've discovered for yourself. Simply deciding to become an options seller because of a perceived built-in edge is not going to make you any money. There's quite a bit more to any winning trading strategy. Given the choice between selling and buying options as a trading vehicle to build a system around, I'll take buying them any day. And so should you. Not because I say so, or because Nassim Taleb got rich on them in the stock market crash of 1987, but because you have already developed a knack for them by learning to beat the binary options contracts consistently. Your foundation has been laid. You know how to find value bets, and you know how important it is not to overpay for any wager relative to the return you are seeking.

Even if 90% of options really do expire worthless, which for the life of me I can't see how, that doesn't mean a thing if the 10% which are worth something on expiration day have an average value that makes up for all the losers. Of course, a strategy built around 90% losers may not be your thing, and who can blame you? My message here is to beware of the strategy that sees 90% winners and then loses it all back plus some on the 10% losers.

You don't have to buy at-the-money options in your trading strategy. I don't. And you probably won't want to, either, for a very good reason – they're expensive. But you probably won't want to sell them, either, for another very good reason – they're risky!

In-the-money options, on the other hand, are cheap. In fact, most options that are $10+ in the money are so cheap they are virtually free. I am obviously speaking of premium price and not the option price. I highly recommend avoiding paying for option premiums over your entire trading career. By premium I mean any amount over what an option is worth in intrinsic value. For example, an option contract that is $10 in the money is worth $10 in intrinsic value. I won't pay more than about $10.20 for one of these, even if it is several months from expiration. The beauty is, I usually don't have to! And these babies make great substitutes for buying or shorting stocks and futures contracts, or even spot currency positions.

Here then is a strategy: Buy $10 in-the-money options for attractive positions you find that are at a support or resistance level, and look poised to move on both the daily and weekly chart. Use an intraday 15-minute chart to find an optimal entry point. Set a stop loss just on the other side of the support/resistance area, like maybe $1 away. As the price moves in your favor, move the stop up an equal distance, but always watch the chart to determine where the best stop and price targets are. You want the stop to be hit when the idea of the trade has obviously failed, but not before. Exit when your stop gets hit or when a reasonable price target at the next support/resistance area is reached and the price stalls noticeably.

Far out-of-the-money options are also cheap, but they are pure premium. I don't like paying for premium. But there is some money to be made with these if you can handle mostly losers while waiting for a few large winners to offset them all. I like out-of-the-money options that cost less than .25. ($25 each). I will buy .05 ($5 options) in many situations. I usually like to have a catalyst, such as a company involved in a takeover bid or accounting scandal. I like to bet the opposite way the news makes you think the price is headed, because those options are cheaper. Obviously, I am betting tiny portions of my account size. Sometimes these will hit for 25 times profit or more when they win, which is a necessary occurrence once in a while for this type of option buying to be profitable.

Of course, you don't have to mess with options at all. There are lots of other ways to trade in the real world, and you can be successful at any of them. The most important thing is to swim with your own personal current, not against it, when deciding what to trade and how to trade it. Go with what you understand, what you have the best aptitude for, and where you feel the most passion.

Converting the Strategies in this Book

Here are suggestions for how the financial betting strategies in this book may convert into brokerage trading methodologies.

Strategy #1: Intraday Breakout. This is a day trading approach, pure and simple. If you prefer the stocks or indices, you should open a margin account at a discount online stock broker – one that has a decent trading platform with streaming intraday charts. For indices, trade the most volatile one in your country (for example the QQQ in the U.S.). Once you are pegged as a pattern day trader you may be unable to use the margin in your account until you have a $25,000 balance. The good news is, at that time you will be given 4x margin for day trading (four times your account balance). Taking full advantage of your day trading buying power will allow you to skyrocket your monthly return from that point forward. Stick to very liquid individual stocks that trade in excess of 1 million shares daily. Get the Trin indicator on your screen and become familiar with it, as trades against the trin are less likely to succeed. If trading overall market breaks only, expect long spells between trades. The QQQ is the single most liquid entity trading more than 100 million shares daily – which means it can effectively be used to trade 25,000 share lots, allowing you to compound your returns until you reach that level.

With currencies, it's a little different. Forex traders enjoy 10x margin or more for all trades, be they day trades or otherwise – even with small account balances. If you are good at intraday breakouts in the Forex markets, you can start earning maximum returns on your account immediately. (Do be careful maxing out your margin, though. A streak of bad trades can really knock you back a ways. I suggest using about one-third of your available buying power per trade for optimum performance trading breakouts.) Currencies are the most liquid entity on the planet and can be used to compound a small day trading account into incredible wealth if you are good – but they tend to be more difficult to master.

Strategy #2: Big Picture Positioning. Options are the only practical vehicle for taking advantage of obvious long-term major trends in gold, oil, and currency pairs. Wait for the first good correction after the new major trend becomes obvious. You can either buy or sell options to take your position. Here selling options isn't such a bad strategy – a credit spread at a level far away the current price will do the trick quite nicely. Let them expire worthless then repeat. If buying options, avoid the expensive at-the-money contracts in favor of cheap in-the-money or out-of-the-money strike prices with several months' time remaining. You will need to open an account at a discount online futures broker. Alternatively, you can just leave a little money in your binary options account for this purpose instead, which might be the most practical solution.

Strategy #3: Reversals. This short-term swing-trading strategy can be worked very easily with a spot currency trading account, individual stocks, or the index ETF's. Use a margin account for stocks and indices and do take full advantage of your margin on every trade. With forex, use about 25% of your available margin. Set good tight stops and use the nearest band as an initial price target, but be prepared to let your outer band positions have the chance of reaching the other outer band. Perhaps close half of your position if it starts trading sideways at the middle band, and the rest if it reverses back towards you. If the trade starts off great but then falls back hard, get out with little or no profit immediately.

You can also use in-the-money options as a trading vehicle. This will increase your leverage considerably in a stock brokerage account (but don't put more than 20% of your account into any one position).

Strategy #4: Straddle and Barrier Range. This is an options trading strategy that has been adopted for binaries, where it works astonishingly well. While the NASDAQ or DAX are the best indices to play this system on at the binary options sites, in a brokerage account you can use it on any of the ETF's or even volatile individual stocks (make sure they are very liquid issues, trading 1 million shares per day or more). The concept is the same: When the market has been quiet, the bet price gets better – which means option premiums get cheaper, and vice-versa.

For straddles, look for quiet non-directional trading over the course of a few days just before important economic numbers are released, or any other potential catalyst. Purchase an at-the-money straddle for the near term month as long as the expiration is more than 3 days away. At-the-money straddles consist of an equal number of calls and puts at the same strike price, which is the nearest strike nearest to the security's current price. Don't pay too much – you should get the whole thing (both sides) for less than 1.50 ($150) total. If the expected move doesn't happen within a couple of days or so, close the position out, win lose or draw. This tactic can work very well on individual stocks the day before earnings are reported, especially with less than two weeks to expiration when time premiums are small. But be aware of pumped-up premiums on stocks that are expected to report "surprise" earnings figures and stay off those plays.

The options equivalent of a Range bet is a *short strangle*. This means selling a call above the current security price at the same time you sell a put below it (usually about the same distance from it). Use the same setup conditions as described in this book. In this situation, you are selling options so you want high premiums. The two strike prices are your range. Make sure you can potentially capture enough premium to justify the risk, and that you are constraining the price within a range that would contain most of the recent price history. If either strike price is breached by more than a smidgeon, close the trade (probably for a loss). The best time to enter these is about three weeks from expiration. When the security's price behaves and expires within the range, you keep all the premium. If the price moves towards one of the strike prices but then reverses back to the middle again, your position will usually become respectably in profit. In this situation, you should close the spread and take your profits if there is still considerable time left.

This strategy can also be used on currencies and commodities in any futures trading account, but it can be difficult to find potential catalysts for the long straddle positions. Make sure you know your market before converting this system to broker-based trading.

Strategy #5: Price Tracking. While the concept of finding value bets holds true for any type of trading (you always want value and never want to overpay for anything), options are the only practical entity for derivative price tracking techniques. Fortunately, options can now be used to trade any liquid market that has at least some spurts of volatility.

A spreadsheet to keep track of option strike prices in various increments above and below your favorite trading vehicles can be handy in hunting for cheap, possibly undervalued options. But if this is your intended strategy, you are going to want to have a few more tools, such as a basic options calculator and perhaps even expensive software such as Option Master or OptionVue. There is a free basic options calculator that does a good job with stocks on the website www.ivolatility.com (They also provide free recommended plays based on value setups they find. Some of these are quite good.) You need to get a good idea as to what the fair value of an option is before you can call it a bargain.

The concept of finding price anomalies is the same as for the strategy taught in this manual. Buy significantly undervalued options no matter which direction they are in, as long as you don't strongly disagree with the technical picture.

Conclusion

Are you ready to take on the trading world? This is a challenging journey that greatly rewards those who make the cut. Most do not. It's primarily a mental and emotional refinement process that will get you there, but one that seems to go against the way we humans are naturally wired. You probably have some re-wiring to do before the floodgates open and the world becomes your oyster.

On the surface, successful trading is quite simple. For example, here's a surefire system: Identify attractive directional trade setups on a chart, enter the trade with a stop loss 1/3 the size of your profit target, and close the trade as soon as either your target or your stop loss is hit. If you are correct 50% of the time in this situation, you are making money. You don't have to worry about a trade hurting you badly because your position size accepts the risk and you are out as soon as your stop gets hit. Heck, it's easy.

That is, as long as your entries have such an edge that you are hitting 50% of them. Your stop is a lot closer than your target, so you better be pretty darn good at predicting direction. Market conditions change, so the same trade setups that are working this month will stop working soon, and then new ones will begin working instead. This is why strategy #4 in this manual is as timeless as it is powerful. You must stay in the ebb and flow of things, constantly reassessing market conditions to find value in the currently-offered derivatives. It's also why robot trading programs fizzle and die. There is no such thing as playing the same trade setup over and over again until you are rich. You have to always be aware of what's happening in the market, switching tactics in reaction, and finding the value plays of today.

But surely you can appreciate how simple the mechanics are. If your trading system depends on 50% winners, such as the scenario just described, you will occasionally see long strings of losers in the distribution of results even as you are working a winning system! That long string of losers, which is to be completely expected sooner or later, will likely cause you to re-evaluate the strategy. Perhaps you will even abandon it completely in search of a new Holy Grail system of some sort. You can blame you? We aren't machines, after all. As emotional humans, we tend to lose faith when things aren't going right. We don't like losses. We can learn to expect a few here and there, but when it gets too lopsided we just can't take it.

That's not to say tinkering with a trading system is never justified. Markets are always changing and it's a good trader who can tweak his strategy to get more in tune with current conditions. But the basic premise remains the same, and losing trades can continue to outpace winners even when positive adjustments have been made which have improved an already-winning system. You just have to ride those periods out. Keep studying, keep fine-tuning what you are doing, and keep the faith. What else are you going to do, give up and not get rich in your life? Hopefully, you will never accept that alternative.

Trade to trade well, not to make money, and the money will take care of itself. Start with a small binary options account and learn to work a strategy or two. When you start making consistent positive returns, begin to add money to your account regularly. Get good with your strategies and don't be afraid to change or incorporate new ones when conditions in your life (or the markets) warrant it.

When you have mastered the fixed odds binaries game – and have a large account balance as a testament to it – move onward and upward to real trading. Take your winning mental fortitude and finely honed skills with you.

About the Author

Drew Kasch is an expert in probability games that are played for money. This includes games which can be beaten such as Poker, Sports Betting, and Blackjack (under certain conditions), games that cannot be beaten such as casino games, and financial probability games such as trading stocks and options. His books will arm you with knowledge and tactics giving you the best chance for success at your chosen area of risk taking. Pick up a Drew Kasch book today and improve your odds!

Visit the Amazon Author page for Drew Kasch at:

www.amazon.com/author/drewkasch

Other Books by Drew Kasch include:

- **How to Milk the Betting Exchange Cash Cow:** See how a handful of sharpies are making 6-figure incomes wagering on everything from bowling to elections

- **How to Shake the Online Poker Money Tree:** Unstoppable Online Poker Strategy for the 21st Century

- **High-Leverage Casino Gambling Systems:** How to play like a minnow and score like a whale on your next casino visit

Made in the USA
Lexington, KY
19 July 2014